Issues in the Digital Age

Online Predators

Carla Mooney

ReferencePoint Press®

San Diego, CA

© 2012 ReferencePoint Press, Inc.
Printed in the United States

For more information, contact:
ReferencePoint Press, Inc.
PO Box 27779
San Diego, CA 92198
www.ReferencePointPress.com

LIBRARY OF CONGRESS CATALOGING-IN-PUBLICATION DATA

Mooney, Carla, 1970–
   Online predators / by Carla Mooney.
      p. cm. — (Issues in the digital age series)
   Includes bibliographical references and index.
   ISBN-13: 978-1-60152-193-4 (hardback)
   ISBN-10: 1-60152-193-6 (hardback)
   1. Internet and teenagers—Juvenile literature. 2. Internet and children—Juvenile literature.
   3. Online sexual predators—Juvenile literature. 4. Internet—Safety measures—Juvenile
   literature. 5. Online chat groups—Safety measures. I. Title.
   HQ799.2.I5M56 2012
   004.67'80835—dc23
                                                                  2011020180

Contents

Introduction

Dangers Online

In 2007 a school resource officer from Birmingham, Alabama, contacted the FBI about a disturbing complaint he had received from one of his high school students. An Internet extortionist was badgering the girl to send nude photos of herself. When FBI agents opened their investigation, they discovered the Internet predator, who went by the username Metascape, had targeted more than 200 young women from several states. After becoming friendly with the women online, Metascape would convince them to send him sexual statements or photos. He then used that material to blackmail the women. In at least 50 cases, Metascape blackmailed his victims into performing graphic sexual acts for him on webcams, which he then used for further blackmail.

A Difficult Case

With the cooperation of law enforcement and victims from several areas, the FBI identified 24-year-old Jonathan Vance from Auburn, Alabama, as the predator. "Tracking him down was complicated. . . . This was really a difficult, unique case,"[1] says Assistant US Attorney Daniel Fortune, who prosecuted the case.

After his arrest, Vance described to FBI investigators some of the methods he used to blackmail the young women and gain control of their Yahoo, Hotmail, Facebook, and MySpace accounts. Sometimes he would contact them through instant messaging and send them a seemingly playful game where he pretended to be a long-lost friend or secret admirer. He told them he would reveal his true identity if they answered 10 questions. He specifically designed the questions to gather intimate and embarrassing personal details about his victims. Sometimes he hacked into a victim's e-mail or Facebook account, using information such as birth date, school, and hometown that he gathered from public

Internet pages. Once Vance controlled the accounts, he gathered more embarrassing details or photos. Then he threatened to expose the photos if the women did not comply with his demands.

For Vance's victims, the fear of discovery often stopped them from telling someone about the predator. "The embarrassment factor was big in this case. How can a girl go to her parents and tell them what happened? Even the adult victim didn't come forward until we contacted her,"[2] says Dale Miskell, supervisory special agent for the FBI cybercrimes squad in Birmingham. Eventually, Vance pleaded guilty to extortion and attempted production of child pornography, among other charges. He was sentenced in April 2009 to 18 years in federal prison.

"Any suspicious activity involving a possible Internet predator should immediately be reported to the FBI or your local police department."[3]

—US attorney Alice Martin.

According to the FBI, Vance's case will be used as an example to train police and prosecutors how to hunt online predators. According to US attorney Alice Martin, Vance's case illustrates the need for people to understand how online predators operate. "Any suspicious activity involving a possible Internet predator should immediately be reported to the FBI or your local police department. All should recognize it isn't a matter of 'if' it will happen, it is 'when,' so youth and adults need to be prepared to identify predators,"[3] she says.

What Is an Online Predator?

When talking about online predators, most people think of sexual offenders such as Vance, who use the Internet to target, groom, and sexually exploit victims. Some online sexual predators are satisfied to keep relationships online. They seek gratification by sending lewd messages to victims via e-mail, instant messaging, or chat rooms. Others want to exchange pornographic photos or webcam links with victims, which can then be forwarded and exchanged with other predators.

Still other sexual predators use the Internet to find victims and eventually attempt to meet them in person. Thirteen-year-old Kylie from Camas, Washington, first met 47-year-old Stanley Sadler on the Internet

Online predators use various ruses to cultivate relationships with potential targets. Tracking down online predators is difficult because computers allow anonymous communication from unidentified locations.

but eventually agreed to meet him in person "I met him in a public place because I wasn't totally stupid. I did get into his car though, because I didn't think we were going to go anywhere. I thought we were just going to talk,"[4] she says. Once he had her in the car, Sadler drove Kylie to a remote parking lot and raped her.

In addition to sexual predators, other types of criminals use the Internet to target and exploit victims in a variety of offenses. Financial predators use the Internet to steal from their victims and commit fraud. One common type of online financial crime occurs when a person purchases a product through a website but then never receives the promised goods or services. Financial predators also use the Internet to steal credit card or bank account information and then use that information to get access to a person's money or to make hundreds or even thousands of dollars in purchases. Some financial predators run online investment or charity frauds, hoping to con an unsuspecting victim into sending them money.

In Tennessee in 2011, a sheriff's deputy described a fake PayPal site, where people were encouraged to pay for online purchases. When a consumer made a $10,000 purchase on the online auction website eBay, he inadvertently went to the fake PayPal site and entered his payment information. Instead of paying for his purchase, the buyer's financial information went straight to the person who had set up the fake site.

In other cases, online predators use the Internet to threaten or bully another person. Cyberbullying can take many forms, from threatening e-mails to Facebook posts designed to humiliate and embarrass a victim. Sometimes the damage done by cyberbullying can be lethal. In 2010 Rutgers University freshman Tyler Clementi committed suicide by jumping off a bridge after his roommate secretly taped and streamed video on the Internet of Clementi in a sexual encounter with another male student.

Hidden Behind a Computer Screen

The Internet allows people to conveniently access information, pay bills, make purchases, and socialize. However, it is also a useful tool for online predators. Using the Internet, online predators can more easily reach a greater number of people in a shorter amount of time. Hidden behind a computer screen, online predators are difficult to detect and identify. For users, knowing the dangers that exist online may help them guard against online predators.

Chapter One

A Real Problem

When 15-year-old Allison arrives home from school, she logs on to the Internet and checks her e-mail for new messages. The Pennsylvania student then begins her homework but leaves her computer on so friends can instant message her about their weekend plans. Her cell phone sits on the desk and beeps each time she receives a new text. Later, Allison logs on to her Facebook account and scrolls through her friends' status updates. Looking forward to a Friday night football game, Allison updates her status to tell her friends where and when to meet. For Allison and her friends, the online world has become a central hub at which to meet, gather, and socialize. They should be careful, however, because it is also a world in which online predators can identify, target, and exploit them.

Revolutionizing Lives

In a few short years the Internet has revolutionized lives. According to a 2010 report by the Pew Internet & American Life Project, 93 percent of American teens between the ages of 12 and 17 regularly go online. The report also found that a large number of adults, 74 percent, use the Internet. So what are all those teens and adults doing online?

For many people like Allison, the Internet has become a place to meet and interact with friends. Gone are the days when teens gathered and hung out after school. Today's teens often have full schedules filled with sports practices, theater rehearsals, extra study sessions, or other activities. Public places such as malls and parks have also adopted rules that limit gatherings of unsupervised teenagers. With less time and opportunity to hang out, teens have turned to the Internet. According to the 2010 Pew report, 73 percent of online teens and 72 percent of online young adults use social networking sites like Facebook. These are the new meeting places.

Instead of talking for hours on the telephone, teens and young adults chat using instant messaging or send quick text messages to each other. They log on to each other's social network profiles to read status updates and view recent pictures. They interact with each other by posting comments on each other's pictures and profiles. On these sites, teens share details of their daily lives, talk about issues that concern them, and plan social events.

In addition to being a social hub, the Internet has become a convenient way for users to find information, go shopping, and pay bills. Instead of driving to the mall to browse through retail stores, people can shop online stores from their homes. According to the Pew report, nearly half (48 percent) of online teens use the Internet to buy things like books, clothing, or music. Adults are even more likely to shop online, with 75 percent reporting that they purchased items online.

In addition to shopping, more people use the Internet to handle their finances. Without being limited by a traditional bank's hours and locations, people pay bills, transfer money between accounts, and buy and sell investments whenever they want from the comfort of their homes. This convenience has transformed online banking into one of the fastest-growing Internet activities. According to a 2009 survey by the Gartner Group, 47 percent of Americans reported that they bank online. "It's pretty hard not to do online banking because it is so convenient, and people want convenience,"[5] says Atul Prakash, a University of Michigan researcher who conducted a study on the risks of Internet banking.

> "The Internet is a dangerous place and just like we teach our children not to converse with strangers on the street and not to run red lights when they're driving, we need to teach children about what to look out for online."[6]
>
> — John Sancin, former president of CyberPatrol.

Evolution of the Internet

The Internet in its earliest days was very different from what exists today. In 1969 the US military funded a research network then named Arpanet. It connected computers at five sites and allowed the computers at each site to "talk" to each other. This system of communication eventually became the Internet.

Online Activities by Age

Percent of Internet users in each generation who engage in this online activity

	0–9%		10–19%		20–29%		30–39%		40–49%
	50–59%		60–69%		70–79%		80–89%		90–100%

Ages 18–33	Ages 34–45	Ages 46–55	Ages 56–64	Ages 65–73	Ages 74+
E-mail	E-mail	E-mail	E-mail	E-mail	E-mail
Search	Search	Search	Search	Search	Search
Health info	Health info	Health info	Health info	Health info	Health info
Social network sites	Get news	Get news	Get news	Get news	Buy a product
Watch video	Gov't website	Gov't website	Gov't website	Travel reservations	Get news
Get news	Travel reservations	Travel reservations	Buy a product	Buy a product	Travel reservations
Buy a product	Watch video	Buy a product	Travel reservations	Gov't website	Gov't website
IM	Buy a product	Watch video	Bank online	Watch video	Bank online
Listen to music	Social network sites	Bank online	Watch video	Financial info	Financial info
Travel reservations	Bank online	Social network sites	Social network sites	Bank online	Religious info
Online classifieds	Online classifieds	Online classifieds	Online classifieds	Rate things	Watch video
Bank online	Listen to music	Listen to music	Financial info	Social network sites	Play games
Gov't website	IM	Financial info	Rate things	Online classifieds	Online classifieds
Play games	Play games	IM	Listen to music	IM	Social network sites
Read blogs	Financial info	Religious info	Religious info	Religious info	Rate things
Financial info	Religious info	Rate things	IM	Play games	Read blogs
Rate things	Read blogs	Read blogs	Play games	Ilsten to music	Donate to charity
Religious info	Rate things	Play games	Read blogs	Read blogs	Listen to music
Online auction	Online auction	Online auction	Online auction	Donate to charity	Podcasts
Podcasts	Donate to charity	Donate to charity	Donate to charity	Online auction	Online auction
Donate to charity	Podcasts	Podcasts	Podcasts	Podcasts	Blog
Blog	Blog	Blog	Blog	Blog	IM
Virtual worlds	Virtual worlds	Virtual worlds	Virtual worlds	Virtual worlds	Virtual worlds

Source: Pew Internet & American Life Project, "Generations 2010: What Different Generations Do Online," December 16, 2010. www.pewinternet.org.

In the 1970s and 1980s people communicated in small groups through closed networks. Telephone lines and modems connected computers physically to the Internet. No home or office personal computers existed. Anyone who used the Internet had to learn a very complicated system. Websites and web pages did not exist. Without a technical background, information was difficult to find. In fact, the early Internet was used primarily by computer experts, engineers, scientists, and librarians.

In addition, because the early Internet was funded by the government, it was initially limited to research, education, and government uses. Commercial uses such as shopping or banking were prohibited. In the 1990s this policy began to change when independent commercial networks developed. Commercial networks made it possible for websites to route traffic from site to site without using the government-funded network.

The introduction of the World Wide Web in 1991 also made using the Internet much easier for the average person. The web was a new system to create, organize, and link documents and web pages so that people could easily read them over the Internet. If the Internet was a system of networks that connected people, the World Wide Web was the means for people to use that connectivity.

The creation of the web browser in the early 1990s further simplified Internet use. Browser software communicated with the Internet and translated web pages into an easy-to-read format on computer screens. Browsers such as Netscape and Internet Explorer helped people of all ages and backgrounds use the Internet.

With the invention of the World Wide Web and web browsers, the Internet grew at a rapid pace. The number of computers connected to the Internet has grown from a few computer scientists to 1.5 billion consumers worldwide.

Web Use Changes

At first people used the Internet passively. They read information but did little to add to it or change what they found online. Around 2002 this pattern of use began to change. People began to use the Internet more interactively. They posted writing, pictures, video, and music on the web. They invited others to view and comment on their sites. They no longer just absorbed the information in front of them. Instead, they created and added their own information.

At the same time, e-commerce exploded on the Internet. Introduced in the mid-1990s, e-commerce is the buying and selling of products or services over the Internet and other computer networks. According to a 2010 report by investment firm J.P. Morgan, global e-commerce was predicted to reach $680 billion in 2011.

As online communication and commerce have become more and more a part of daily life, a variety of predators have seen opportunities that never existed before. Hiding behind an anonymous computer screen, people with malicious intent use the Internet every day to find and exploit victims.

Real Risks

While the Internet offers numerous advantages and conveniences, it has opened the door to many real risks. Eager to connect on social networks or shop online, people may let their guard down and share with strangers information that could be used to hurt them. Sexual predators lurk in chat rooms and social networking sites, looking for potential victims. Financial predators send fake e-mails, hack into computers, or develop elaborate online frauds to access a victim's bank account, credit cards, or Social Security number. Cyberbullies use social networking sites to post humiliating pictures or comments or send threatening texts. "The Internet is a dangerous place and just like we teach our children not to converse with strangers on the street and not to run red lights when they're driving, we need to teach children about what to look out for online,"[6] says John Sancin, president of CyberPatrol, a company that develops web-monitoring software.

Some of the Internet's characteristics make people more vulnerable to online predators. Once information or pictures are posted on the Internet, they can be accessed and searched indefinitely. Material found

"Unfortunately, cybercriminals are among the most adept at leveraging these new technologies, and have embraced the Internet to facilitate their criminal behavior."[10]

— Linda Criddle, Internet child-safety expert and author.

Please Rob Me

Although social networking sites and location-based apps have made it easy for users to tell friends where they are and what they are doing, sharing personal information online also makes it easier for would-be thieves to plan their next heist. Status posts and pictures tell criminals if a potential victim is on vacation or out for the evening, if they have a dog, and if they own fancy cars or big televisions. In 2009 a group of thieves was arrested near Los Angeles, California, for a series of burglaries targeting celebrities. According to police, the thieves used Internet mapping and gossip sites to case their targets' homes.

A website called PleaseRobMe.com is drawing attention to the risks of sharing locations online. The site has accumulated public posts from location-based services such as Foursquare or Gowalla that allow users to check in to places like restaurants, bars, and stores and then broadcast their location to their online friends. The site allows users to filter the posts by geographic location. According to the founders, the site's goal is to raise awareness and have people think more carefully about unintended consequences when they broadcast their location on the Internet.

online can be forwarded, copied, or pasted anywhere. In addition, every online post is open not only to intended viewers but also to anyone else who happens to be wandering through the online landscape; users never know who is reading or seeing what they post online. A blog update or credit card number intended for a select few could easily be viewed by more than the intended audience. In addition, the ability to connect without seeing or hearing the other person can sometimes cause inhibitions to break down. People are more likely to be uncivil or downright nasty in an anonymous e-mail, blog post, or social media comment than they would be face-to-face.

Portrait of an Online Predator

Because the Internet masks a user's identity, spotting online predators is often difficult. They can be located in almost any city or country, and they can be any age, race, gender, or nationality. Because the Internet connects computers globally, online predators may even live in a different country. They may act alone or in loosely organized groups. Other times, online predators operate within the structure of organized criminal gangs.

While online predators could be anyone, in the case of sexual predators, investigators have found that the vast majority of offenders, 95 percent, are male. In addition, a 2009 report by the University of New Hampshire's Crimes Against Children Research Center found that online sexual offenders are getting younger. Young adult offenders, aged 18 to 25, rose from 23 percent in 2000 to 40 percent of arrests in 2006. The report's authors suggest this shift may have happened because "adults aged 18 to 25 may be more likely than older adults to use the Internet when engaged in deviant behavior."[7]

In addition to online predators who directly commit crimes, another type of online criminal, the middleman, has emerged. Middlemen use the Internet to collect personal data, including names, addresses, Social Security numbers, and credit card details of victims. Then they compile the stolen information into virtual catalogs and sell it to anyone willing to pay. Middlemen frequently turn to underground economy servers or black market forums to sell their stolen information. These places are typically chat servers on which stolen data is bought and sold. According to the 2010 Symantec Internet Security Threat Report, credit card numbers were the most common item for sale in these black market forums, with bank account numbers, e-mail accounts, attack tools, and e-mail addresses rounding out the top five items for sale.

Who Is Vulnerable?

Anyone who goes online is at risk of being victimized by an online predator. Computer protections such as antivirus software, firewalls, and content filters are useless if a user responds to a fake e-mail or Internet fraud and willingly provides personal or confidential information. According to Gartner, Inc., an information technology research and advisory company, more than 5 million US consumers lost money to phishing attacks that tricked users into handing over personal information in the 12 months ended September 2008. This was an almost 40 percent increase over the number of victims in the previous 12-month period.

Teens and young adults are especially at risk of being victimized by an online predator. They spend a lot of time online and often have a false sense of security about their online communications. In addition, around the age of 13 to 15, teens begin to reach out and form relationships with people outside their family and close circle of friends. The Internet has become a convenient avenue for teens looking for approval or rebelling against parental control. Teens may not recognize the warning signs of an online predator. Online predators know the vulnerability of this group and are prepared to take advantage of teens. "They're not only very manipulative, they are also very good at finding a weakness in

A bulletin board filled with mug shots of online predators hangs in a Pennsylvania detective agency. Investigators say most online predators are male. Some act alone while others work within loosely structured groups or in organized gangs.

that child and exploit it. They're looking for a kid starved for time, attention, love, and affection,"[8] says Brad Russ of the Department of Justice Internet Crimes Against Children Task Force.

How Big Is the Problem?

More than 2 billion people worldwide use the Internet through cell phones and computers and other devices that allow online access. In the United States, 93 percent of teens aged 12 to 17 and 74 percent of adults 18 years old or older go online. While all these people chat, socialize, and shop online, many have become targets for criminals. "Criminals are opportunists. Wherever you have lots of people, they'll see lots of opportunities,"[9] says Charles Pavelites, a supervisory special agent at the Internet Crime Complaint Center, a partnership between the FBI, the National White Collar Crime Center, and the Bureau of Justice Assistance.

Online predators have been successful at finding opportunities for turning targets into victims. According to the Crimes Against Children Research Center, one in five US teenagers who regularly logs on to the Internet says that he or she has received an unwanted sexual solicitation via the web. A 2010 report from *Consumer Reports* showed that 1 million households have been the victim of e-mail frauds or phishing, costing an estimated total of $650 million dollars in 2010 alone. In addition, cyberbullying among teens is a pervasive problem. According to a 2010 research study by the Pew Internet & American Life Project, nearly one in three, or 32 percent, of online teens experienced some form of online harassment. "The Internet provides unparalleled opportunities for instant access to information and helpful services. Unfortunately, cybercriminals are among the most adept at leveraging these new technologies, and have embraced the Internet to facilitate their criminal behavior,"[10] writes Lindle Criddle, an Internet child-safety expert and author.

Online Roadmap for Predators

Sometimes individual actions are the greatest threat to a person's online safety. Users often unknowingly leak valuable identity information through social media status updates, photos, or other information. Even an e-mail address can give away personal information. For example, the address Lily16diver@network.com gives clues to a person's name, age, and hobbies. These small details might be enough for a predator to start a conversation with the user.

Teens in particular post a variety of information about themselves and their daily routines that can help predators identify and target them. "Every piece of information about you is a valuable commodity. Publically available user information has the potential to be tracked, catalogued, analyzed, and sold, both legally and illegally,"[11] writes Criddle. Sometimes, this information can seem harmless, like eye color or a person's mood. Yet those details, along with a few other key pieces of information such as name, address, and age, can help a predator impersonate, steal from, or contact a user. Pictures that show the name of a school, street, or sports team can be used to determine a user's location, habits, interests, age, and more. Once predators have that information, they can do anything they want with it. They can sell it to other predators. They can open up a credit card in a user's name or steal money from a bank account. They could also rob a victim's house or try to meet a victim in person.

> "Kids would never hand out their name and address to a stranger in the real world, so it's alarming to see how many kids do that very thing online."[12]
>
> — Tracy Mooney, a McAfee Cyber Security expert.

Social network sites are usually rich with personal information. A 2007 study by the Pew Internet & American Life Project found that 82 percent of social network profile creators included their first name in their profiles and 79 percent have included photos of themselves. Sixty-one percent of teens on social networking sites included the name of their city or town in their profile and 49 percent included the name of their school. "Kids know not to talk to strangers—it's one of the first lessons you teach them. However, online, there's a sense of trust and anonymity, so kids let their guard down. Kids would never hand out their name and address to a stranger in the real world, so it's alarming to see how many kids do that very thing online,"[12] says Tracy Mooney, a McAfee Cyber Security expert.

Social Networks

Social networking refers to two or more people communicating. Online social networking can take the form of a blog, chat room discussion, instant messaging, discussion board posts, e-mail, and social network posts. A user's trusted network is made up of the people he or she knows personally and trusts outside of the online world. A casual network is much broader and includes people whom the user has not met in person and does not know or trust.

Potential problems arise in social networking when users blur the lines between trusted networks and casual networks. A user may have no way of knowing if an online person is telling the truth unless the user knows that person in the offline world. Users also overestimate their Internet anonymity. Through posts and pictures, they give unintentional clues to the casual network about their location, hobbies, and interests. Even when users limit their online interactions to a trusted network, a friend can forward or repost the information, making it available to a larger and unintended audience. Every day, new stories appear about people who have been stalked by someone they met online, had their identity stolen, or have been bullied online. So while social networking can make it easier to stay in touch with friends and family, it also can increase a user's exposure to people who have less-than-honorable intentions.

Safety Efforts May Not Be Enough

Even more troubling, online safety education may not be enough to protect users from giving away sensitive information online. A 2008 study by AOL found that 89 percent of Internet users have willingly given away personal details online even though they understood the risks of doing so. "Our research identified a significant gap between what people say and what they do when it comes to protecting sensitive information online,"[13] says Jules Polonetsky, AOL's chief privacy officer.

No matter how careful users are when online, their personal data can be leaked by other people, companies, or the government. For example, Social Security numbers of millions of Americans, a gold mine for online financial predators, can be found on websites that offer access to public documents. Although the federal courts banned Social Security numbers from appearing on public documents in 2001, older documents may still have them. A Virginia state senator discovered that his and his wife's Social Security numbers were printed near the bottom of their home's property deed and posted online after they refinanced their mortgage. "I was shocked, and I briefly flipped out, because, you know, these are days when everybody's privacy is under assault,"[14] says State Senator Jaime Raskin. "This is very dangerous," said Maryland attorney general Douglas Gansler after learning that his own number had been posted on a Maryland government records site. "You know, a Social Security number is really the fingerprint to somebody's identification."[15]

> "Our research identified a significant gap between what people say and what they do when it comes to protecting sensitive information online."[13]
>
> — Jules Polonetsky, America Online's chief privacy officer.

Risk Versus Reward

The Internet has revolutionized life around the world. It has changed the way people communicate, buy products, find information, and entertain themselves. According to a 2008 report by the Digital Youth Project at the University of California at Berkeley, "The digital world is creating new opportunities for youth to grapple with social norms, explore interests, develop technical skills, and experiment with new forms of self-expression."[16] Possibilities in the online world appear to be endless.

At the same time, the power of the Internet has also been harnessed by criminals, making it a potentially dangerous place for the unaware and unprotected. Financial criminals, sexual predators, scam artists, and cyberbullies lurk on the web looking for the next unsuspecting victim. These predators have become very skilled at using the Internet to hide their real identity and intent. "The problem of online predators, from pedophiles to child pornographers to cyber bullies, is getting worse,"[17] says Bob Bales, president of CyberPatrol.

Chapter Two

Sexual Predators

When Katie was 15 years old, she began talking to people in an on-line chat room, including a 22-year-old man named Jon. Before long, Jon asked Katie if she wanted to talk on the phone. "I thought, He lives all the way across the country—what's the worst that could happen? We ended up talking for five hours straight. Two days later, we were boyfriend and girlfriend,"[18] says Katie, whose story appears in the December 2009 *Human Sexuality Newsletter*.

During the next few months, Jon carefully groomed Katie. He claimed to have the same music interests, sent her gifts, and made her feel guilty when she hung out with her friends instead of chatting or talking with him. Before long, Jon bought a plane ticket to visit Katie. When she told her parents about the upcoming meeting, they immediately were concerned. Katie's dad talked to a police officer who recommended a computer game called *Missing*, which simulates how online predators operate. "Once I started playing, I realized the predator in the game was doing and saying a lot of the same things as Jon. . . . Red flags started waving in my head,"[19] said Katie.

When Katie tried to break off her relationship with Jon, he filled her e-mail inbox with messages. The police investigated and quickly discovered that Jon was wanted by the FBI for raping a 13-year-old girl. Jon was arrested, and Katie testified at his trial about how he used the Internet to lure her. With the help of her testimony, Jon was convicted and sentenced to 20 years in prison.

What Is an Online Sexual Predator?

There are many different types of online sexual predators. Some, like Jon, use the Internet to develop a relationship with a victim and then try to extend that relationship into the real world. They might exchange phone numbers and talk to their victim on the phone. They might also send pictures of themselves and ask their victim to send photos. Most are good at manipulating victims. Eventually, they suggest meeting in person. Some buy plane or bus tickets for their victims to come visit them. Some may even be up front about their intentions and suggest a sexual activity.

Other sexual predators are interested in keeping their online relationship online. They may want to collect and trade child pornography pictures and videos. Others are excited by online sexual conversations and a victim's reaction to their comments.

Sexual predators also use the Internet to connect with other predators. Online, they can exchange child pornography. In chat rooms and online forums, they can brag anonymously about conquests or give tips for grooming victims. They can also exchange tips to avoid being caught. In March 2011 European police busted a major online pedophile ring, arresting more than 100 people. The ring operated in an online forum

A Massachusetts police detective arrests a man alleged to be an online sexual predator. Sexual predators often target teenage girls or boys by first developing online relationships and then sometimes requesting photos and personal information or even setting up a face-to-face meeting.

where people shared their interest in young boys. "Having made contact on the site, some members would move to more private channels, such as email, to exchange and share illegal images and films of children being abused,"[20] state Europol investigators in a press release.

Finding Victims

The Internet has made it easier for sexual predators to find potential victims. Hiding behind an anonymous screen name, a predator can pretend to be anyone to gain a victim's trust and develop a relationship. Connecting people around the globe, the Internet offers a great number of potential targets for the predator, many more than could be reached in person.

According to Carol Smolenski, director of ECPAT (End Child Prostitution and Trafficking), online child pornography and exploitation have become a billion-dollar business. Every day, a child or teen is being victimized online. "You no longer have to wear a raincoat and find a spot at the playground where you can flash somebody. You can sit in the presumed privacy of your own home or office, or in a library or an Internet cafe, and find chat rooms and blogs and e-mail and do all kinds of things to avail yourself to hundreds of thousands of victims that you would not otherwise have access to,"[21] says Deputy District Attorney Maryann Grippo of Pennsylvania's Lackawanna County.

To identify targets, sexual predators surf the Internet, often browsing personal profiles that teens post on social networking sites. Research has found that most Internet sex crimes involve adult men who use the Internet to meet and seduce underage adolescents into sexual encounters. They look for vulnerabilities such as insecurity, unhappiness, loneliness, or risk-taking. Teens who post photos of themselves, give a physical description, and include name, age, sex, and location in their profile are more likely targets. "It's one-stop shopping. You have the profile and instant messaging right there. These networking sites are a perfect predator's playground . . . they can troll through and look for pretty faces that they like and get all the information they

> "These networking sites are a perfect predator's playground . . . they can troll through and look for pretty faces that they like and get all the information they want."[22]
>
> — Monique Nelson, executive vice president of Web Wise Kids, a nonprofit Internet safety organization.

Online Gaming

Video game systems such as Xbox, PlayStation, and Wii have become a new place for online sexual predators to find victims. These systems, which are popular with kids and adults alike, enable players to connect online to other players all around the world. Players can talk to each other online, play games, and make friends. Some gamers use their home computers or even their cell phones to play online games. While online gaming can be a great way to socialize and learn strategy, it can also be an easy place for sexual predators to find victims.

A fan of online gaming, Erica McWhorter experienced first-hand how online predators operate in the gaming world. In an interview with a Denver investigative reporter, she said that one day while she was playing on her Xbox, another gamer sent her instant messages with personal questions. He asked if she was a girl, how old she was, and if she had a webcam. Then the gamer asked McWhorter if she wanted to see his private parts.

According to the FBI, overtures from sexual predators through online gaming are fast-growing crimes. Online sexual predators may send nude pictures or arrange sexual meetings with teens they meet while gaming. According to Mike Harris, an investigator with the district attorney's office in Jefferson County, California, kids and teens are contacted through online games more frequently than parents realize. He says that is not surprising because sex offenders will go anywhere kids and teens go.

want,"[22] says Monique Nelson, executive vice president of Web Wise Kids, a nonprofit Internet safety organization.

Online sexual predators also lurk anonymously in chat rooms, looking for victims who have regular access to a computer. Being online frequently may mean a victim has few outside interests, which makes him or her more attractive to a predator. Potential targets who use instant messaging are also more attractive, because instant messages leave fewer traces than e-mail messages, which must be deleted.

A 2007 study of 31 convicted Internet sex offenders found that 81 percent used chat rooms to identify and contact potential victims. More than half of those tried to set up an in-person meeting for sex with victims they had met in chat rooms. Almost half of the offenders, or 48 percent, also used online profiles to screen for potential victims.

When asked what attracted the study offenders to their victims, three themes emerged. First, if users mentioned sex in any way, whether through online comments or in provocative user names or e-mail addresses, the predator would try to contact them. Second, being needy or submissive online attracted the attention of predators. One study participant said, "Neediness is very apparent when a child will do anything to keep talking to you. Also that they are always online shows a low sense of parental contact or interest in the child."[23] Finally, if the user's screen name sounded young, such as Sarah15, it prompted predators to initiate contact.

Grooming Victims

Once a sexual predator identifies a target online, he grooms the victim. One of the first things a predator tries to do is build trust with the victim. Predators learn their victims' habits and what they like and dislike. Reading social networking profiles and blogs or following chat room conversations can easily give the predator these answers. "The police we work with tell us that when a predator starts grooming a child, he looks for vulnerability, and with a diary or blog right there, he's already gotten past the first stage,"[24] says Nelson.

Predators understand that many teens use the Internet to vent or talk about what is going on in their life. Many are simply looking for a person who will listen, commiserate, and understand. Predators take advantage of this desire and use attention, affection, and sometimes gifts to make victims feel special and as if they "owe" the predator for showing such compassion.

Another important way that a sexual predator grooms his victim is to drive a wedge between the victim and his or her family and friends. Predators can more easily control people who feel isolated, and someone in that position is less likely to ask for help or report a problem. Sometimes an online predator will blackmail or threaten to tell a victim's family about their relationship if the victim does not continue to do what he demands.

As a summer camp counselor in North Carolina, 27-year-old Jason Betensky used online social networking sites to learn more about his campers. After camp ended, he contacted several campers online, sometimes pretending to be a young female or another camper. Betensky used information that he learned on the Internet and while at camp to make his ruse appear legitimate. Once he started an online relationship with a camper, Betensky would then try to convince the camper to send him sexually explicit pictures or videos of herself. Once Betensky received something incriminating, he used it to blackmail his victim for more sexual material. If the victim tried to end her relationship with him, he threatened to expose the pictures and videos to her friends and family. Eventually, police arrested Betensky in September 2010 after he had victimized at least nine campers.

Predators like Betensky have become extremely proficient at using the Internet to find and groom victims. Samantha Wilson, a retired Canadian police officer and expert in Internet sex crimes, says that

Various efforts are underway to crack down on sexual predators. Alicia Kozakiewicz, center, was abducted by a sexual predator as a teenager. She has urged lawmakers to adopt a bill that provides more funding for efforts to stop sexual predators who prey on young people.

Alicia's Law

Protecting Virginia Families from Online Predators and Child Pornographe

✓ Expand Internet Crimes Against Children Task Forces ($3.8 million)

✓ Capacity-building grants to local law enforcement agencies ($4.5 million)

✓ 3 new dedicated forensic crime labs ($6 million)

✓ New prosecutors and training ($1.5 million)

✓ Internet safety education

A Teaching Tool

Several computer games can help teens learn about the dangers of online predators and cyberbullying. Web Wise Kids, a nonprofit organization that teaches kids and teens about online safety, developed the popular game *Missing*. *Missing* is based on the true story of a boy who was lured by an online sexual predator. In the game, players work with a detective to find and rescue the boy and arrest the predator. By using language and tricks commonly used by online sexual predators, *Missing* helps teens recognize the warning signs of an online predator.

Mirror Image, another game created by Web Wise Kids, tells the story of two teens who are victimized by a predator who uses the Internet to lure young women with promises of modeling contracts and online romances. The teens do not realize that the predator has hacked into their computers and loaded spyware onto their computers. Players work with police to track the predator and arrest him.

Schools around the country have used *Missing* and *Mirror Image* to educate students about the dangers of online predators.

behavior like Betensky's has become so common that it has a specific name: sextortion. "I wish it wasn't as common as it has become. When children are on-line, there really is a disconnect between the technology and the reality, and kids really don't get it,"[25] says Wilson.

Task Forces Fight Online Sexual Predators

While sexual predators use the Internet to target and groom victims, law enforcement is also moving online to stop them. Many agencies and police departments have set up task forces to investigate suspected offenders. Investigators pose as teens and e-mail or chat with potential predators until they gather enough evidence to make an arrest.

Police detective Chris Shermer from the Missoula, Montana, Internet Crimes Against Children Task Force frequently poses as a teen in Internet chat rooms. "I watch a lot of Nickelodeon,"[26] says Shermer, explaining how he so convincingly impersonates a teenage girl online. As a full-time member of the task force, Shermer works daily from a computer in a basement office. Kids generally go online at night and after school between 3:30 and 5:30 p.m. That is when the predators come out, looking for potential targets. Shermer is online too, joining the chat room conversations. Shermer keeps typing until a predator decides he wants to meet the young teen he thinks Shermer is.

In one June 2010 case, Shermer posed as a 14-year-old girl. After chatting online for a while, a high school girls' basketball coach arranged a liaison with Shermer. The coach promised to bring the "girl" to his home for sex and offered to buy condoms before the meeting. Instead, Shermer's team arrested him.

> "The police we work with tell us that when a predator starts grooming a child, he looks for vulnerability, and with a diary or blog right there, he's already gotten past the first stage."[24]
>
> — Monique Nelson, executive vice president of Web Wise Kids, a nonprofit Internet safety organization.

Internet Crimes Against Children Task Force

Launched in 1998, the Internet Crimes Against Children Task Force Program (ICAC) is a national network of 61 coordinated task forces that represent more than 3,000 federal, state, and local law enforcement agencies across the country. The ICAC program provides federal grants to help these agencies find, arrest, and prosecute online sexual predators. The program was developed when law enforcement noted the increasing number of children and teens using the Internet, the easy spread of pornography online, and increased Internet use by predators searching for victims. The program also helps state and local law enforcement agencies with training, technical assistance, victim services, and community education.

In South Carolina, Attorney General Henry McMaster announced in November 2010 that the state's ICAC task force had arrested 200 suspected Internet predators since April 2004. "This milestone in our fight against Internet child predators in South Carolina is a testament to the professionalism and dedication of the seventy-seven law enforcement officers in the state that work in daily cooperation with each other to make this task force a success," said McMaster in his announcement recognizing the achievement. "However, this day highlights a very dangerous problem in our state—that adults are constantly on the Internet seeking to harm our children. No matter how many predators are caught in our sting operations, we are confident that there are scores of children hurt that we never know anything about,"[27] McMaster warned.

Innocent Images National Initiative

The FBI, in addition to local and state law enforcement agencies, also investigates online sexual predators. In the mid-1990s FBI agents investigating sexual predators noted that offenders were routinely using computers to send sexually explicit images to minors and to lure minors into illicit sexual activity. As a result, the FBI launched the Innocent Images National Initiative (IINI). Managed by the FBI's Cyber Division in Washington, DC, the IINI provides a coordinated FBI response to online sexual predators. In 2007 IINI cases were 39 percent of all investigations worked by the FBI's Cyber Division.

Working undercover, FBI agents use fake screen names and engage in online chat or e-mail conversations with potential offenders, looking for evidence of criminal activity. IINI operations are also coordinated with ICAC task forces. Sometimes the IINI becomes involved in a case because of a citizen tip or a referral from a law enforcement agency. Other times, the name of an online location such as a chat room suggests illicit activity and can draw the attention of agents.

Entrapment

When task force detectives go online, they usually pose as teens, deceiving potential predators. Under the law, investigators are allowed to use some deception, but they cannot persuade a person to commit a crime that he or she had no intention of committing. For example, a police officer could pretend to be someone online and offer to engage in an illicit activity. A potential offender who readily accepts can be arrested. If it appears that the potential offender did not intend to commit the crime and only did so with persuasion from the police officer, the courts may rule that the police entrapped the alleged offender.

For task force officers working online sexual predator cases, keeping the balance between legal deception and entrapment can be tricky. In one case near Philadelphia, a task force officer pretended to be the mother of two young girls. In an online chat room, she pretended to be interested in arranging for a man to have sexual contact with her daughters. The investigator identified a potential predator, "J," and chatted with him online for months. According to "J," he was only interested in having sex with the adult woman but talked about activity with her daughters to keep her interested in him. When he arrived at the meeting place, police were waiting to arrest him. "I know I have no sexual interest in children at all . . . I certainly had no intention of doing it. I intended to have sex with her and then leave. Period,"[28] he told a *Vanity Fair* reporter who profiled his case in December 2009.

> "The only way you can teach students responsible Internet use is to demonstrate responsible Internet use. If it's all blocked, they don't ever learn anything."[38]
>
> — Steven Anderson, a district instructional technologist in North Carolina.

In practice, predators often have difficulty proving they were entrapped by police. Most people and juries find it hard to believe that law enforcement planted a criminal idea in the mind of a law-abiding citizen and prompted that person to act on it. "The people who are out there trolling and looking, by the language that they use, most of them sort of seal their own fate,"[29] says Roanoke defense attorney Deborah Caldwell-Bono.

Joining the Fight

In addition to law enforcement and task forces, Internet service providers (ISPs) have joined the fight against online predators. In July 2008 several of the largest US Internet providers, including AT&T and America Online, announced that they had eliminated access to online discussion groups that feature child pornography. Prior to the ban, users had been able to post messages in these newsgroups for each other to read. Investigators in the

New York State attorney general's office found that 88 different newsgroups contained more than 11,000 lewd pictures of minors.

In addition, social networking sites such as Facebook and MySpace are using computer code to track online sexual predators. MySpace developed software that automatically searches through the site's more than 100 million profiles and identifies registered sex offenders. "We have zero tolerance for sexual predators on MySpace and took the initiative to create this first of its kind tool ourselves because nothing previously existed," says Hemanshu Nigam, MySpace's chief security officer. "We will continue to promote legislation requiring sex offenders to register their e-mail addresses so they can be kept off social networking sites in the first place."[30] In 2009 Connecticut attorney general Richard Blumenthal announced that MySpace had identified and kicked off 90,000 sex offenders over the previous two years. "These convicted, registered sex offenders clearly create profiles seeking to prey on children,"[31] he said.

Facebook has also adopted a zero tolerance policy for online sexual predators. "Our policy has been to remove convicted sex offenders when they are reported or identified through any means,"[32] says Chris Kelly, Facebook's chief privacy officer. Kelly says the convicted sexual offenders on the site were found through user reports, working with local law enforcement agencies, and using the national sex offender registry. Through these efforts, Facebook removed more than 5,000 convicted sex offenders from its site between May 2008 and January 2009. "The message in this number is Facebook has an equal stake in solving this problem of protecting children. They [Facebook] have an equal stake in the predator problem and its solution,"[33] says Blumenthal, who along with North Carolina attorney general Roy Cooper has led an effort to remove sex offenders from social networking sites.

In addition, both Facebook and MySpace have implemented dozens of safeguards designed to protect minors from online sexual predators. Some of these safeguards include limiting older users' ability to search for minors and building a task force to seek ways to better verify users' ages and identities. "Social networks that encourage kids to come to their sites have a responsibility to keep those kids safe. We've now gotten the two largest social networking sites to agree to take significant steps to protect children from predators and pornography,"[34] says Cooper.

Fighting Online Predators at Home

Despite the efforts of law enforcement and online sites, the best defense against online sexual predators often begins at home. Public education campaigns inform users how online sexual predators operate and ways they can stay safe online. One such group, Stop Child Predators,

Law enforcement agencies in New Hampshire release an Internet safety guide to help families protect children and teens from online sexual predators. Public education is considered an important tool in the fight against sexual predators.

launched a public education campaign in July 2008 to increase awareness of emerging Internet technologies, educate parents and communities about online threats, and empower them to protect their online safety and privacy. "By increasing awareness, Stop Internet Predators seeks to limit the potential for child predators to abuse online technologies to prey on children,"[35] says Stacie Rumenap, executive director of Stop Child Predators.

At home, users can also install filtering and monitoring software on computers. Depending on the program, monitoring programs can block or restrict chat room activity. Some programs block and restrict access to certain sites, such as chat rooms or instant messaging programs, while others monitor and record what a computer user does online.

Responsibility Lines Blurred

While many people work to make the online world safer for users, there is debate over who holds the primary responsibility for minors' online safety. Some believe that the primary responsibility to keep teens safe online begins with parents and teens. According to Kelly, social networks should help protect minors who use the sites, but parents must also be held accountable for their children's safety. "There are multiple layers of responsibility and the core for us is to provide the tools that will be effective at protecting kids," says Kelly. He believes that basic Internet safety education begins at home. "One of the things that you have to do is educate kids not to meet anyone that they only know online, and to tell their parents where they're going and what they're doing, and have the parents be an active participant in their lives,"[36] Kelly says.

Yet even the most diligent parents cannot control access to online sites outside of their home. Many teens use computers daily at schools and libraries or have Internet access on their cell phones. Recognizing the potential for problems, many high schools have developed comprehensive Internet use policies. These policies include restricting cell phone use, blocking access to certain sites, and monitoring student Internet activity on school grounds.

Some educators believe that blocking access to sites does not teach teens to use the Internet safely. Tom Whitby, an adjunct professor of English education at St. Joseph's College in New York, thinks that instead of blocking sites, school districts should teach students how to behave online and talk to them about online risks and benefits. "If you're teaching them at an early age, you don't have to worry about blocking because they understand the do's and don'ts,"[37] Whitby says. Steven Anderson, a district instructional technologist in North Carolina agrees. "The only way you can teach students responsible Internet use is to demonstrate responsible Internet use. If it's all blocked, they don't ever learn anything,"[38] says Anderson.

An Exaggerated Problem?

Some people believe that the problem of online sexual predators has been exaggerated by the media. A task force led by the Berkman Center for Internet and Society at Harvard University concluded in 2009 that the problem is not as significant as many have been led to believe. In its report, the task force noted that children and teenagers were unlikely to be propositioned by adults online. When it did happen, the task force found that the teens were usually willing participants who already had risk factors such as poor home environments or substance abuse problems. The report found that online bullying was a far more serious problem than online sexual solicitation of minors by adults. "The vast majority of kids in this country have heard the messages about the risks online and are basically dealing with them as a nuisance, as a fact of life, and aren't particularly vulnerable," says Ernie Allen, president of the National Center for Missing and Exploited Children. He did caution, "This report should not be read as saying there are not adults out there doing this."[39]

> "Rapid technological advances with mobile phones, PDAs, video gaming systems and online social networking sites place our children more at risk from predators than at any time before. Our arrest rate is only limited by the amount of resources."[40]
>
> — Henry McMaster, South Carolina's attorney general.

Some officials are disturbed by the report's findings. They argue that it gives users a false sense of security when in fact online predators are more dangerous than ever. "Rapid technological advances with mobile phones, PDAs, video gaming systems and online social networking sites place our children more at risk from predators than at any time before. Our arrest rate is only limited by the amount of resources,"[40] says McMaster.

Like many new technologies, the Internet carries both risk and reward. "The Internet is a wonderful tool that has transformed and improved the lives of millions of people. Unfortunately, sexual predators have also made it a dangerous weapon that can be used to victimize innocent children,"[41] says New York State senator Joseph E. Robach.

Chapter Three

Financial Predators

When Janis Stuart, a retired San Diego personal trainer, returned from vacation in April 2010, she turned on her home computer and checked her e-mail. In one message, Stuart's bank notified her that per her instructions all future e-mails would be sent to a new e-mail address. Because Stuart had never notified her bank of an e-mail change, she visited her local bank branch. "My immediate reaction was that they had confused accounts, and this was a big mistake,"[42] she said. At the bank, a clerk told Stuart that approximately $5,800 was about to be transferred from her savings account to a woman that Stuart did not know. Stuart immediately instructed the bank to stop the payment.

Bank officials told Stuart that her computer had probably been infected with a virus that allowed a financial predator to steal passwords to her online bank account. The would-be thief then changed her e-mail address and initiated the bill payment. The bank authorized the changes because the hacker knew the answers to Stuart's secret questions—such as her mother's maiden name and where she was born. (Keystroke tracking software might be one way for hackers to obtain this type of information.) "It was a fluke that I caught it in time before the money disappeared. I was very upset,"[43] said Stuart.

Internet Opens New Doors for Theft

As more people go online to shop, bank, and do business, stories like Stuart's have become increasingly common. Financial predators search online for an opportunity to swindle unsuspecting victims. While most people know not to give out their credit card or Social Security numbers to strangers, they might unknowingly divulge that same personal information online. Moreover, because banks and retailers store customers' personal information electronically, data breaches on their computer networks make customers vulnerable to financial predators. In 2010 the FBI's Internet Crime Complaint Center received more than 300,000 complaints of online financial fraud, an average of about 25,000 complaints per month.

Before the Internet, financial predators stole wallets and credit cards. They used the mail or telephone to con people out of their money. Most criminals operated in a specific geographical area with a limited number of potential targets. Because the Internet connects so many people around the world it has given financial predators access to people thousands of miles away.

> "Using anonymous e-mails, short-lived Web sites, and falsified domain name registrations, many fraud operators are able to strike quickly, victimize thousands of consumers in a short period of time and disappear without a trace."[44]
>
> —Eric L. Carlson, editor at the *Elder Law Journal.*

The anonymous nature of the Internet also makes it easier for financial predators to operate. They hide behind a computer screen and pretend to be a legitimate person or business. Before anyone realizes the online ruse, they can defraud thousands of people and then seemingly vanish. "Using anonymous e-mails, short-lived Web sites, and falsified domain name registrations, many fraud operators are able to strike quickly, victimize thousands of consumers in a short period of time and disappear without a trace,"[44] writes Eric L. Carlson, an editor at the *Elder Law Journal.*

How Financial Predators Work Online

Financial predators use many tactics to defraud people online. They may pretend to be a bank and trick a victim into e-mailing personal information such as passwords, Social Security, or credit card numbers. They may develop a computer virus that infects a victim's computer. Some viruses unleash spyware, malicious programs that gather keystroke information without the user's knowledge. Alternatively, financial predators may pretend to be a vendor selling a fake product.

The FBI's Internet Fraud Complaint Center has received hundreds of thousands of financial fraud complaints resulting from Internet scams. The US attorney general at the time, Janet Reno (right), announces the center's creation in 2000. It continues to operate today.

Regardless of method, the main goal of financial predators is to steal money or other valuable items.

According to a 2011 FBI report, the most common type of online financial fraud is nondelivery of merchandise or payment. This usually happens when someone poses as an online merchant, who offers to sell a product, such as a television. Once the customer sends payment, the so-called merchant disappears and never delivers the promised product. This type of fraud can also occur when the predator poses as a buyer. Established businesses usually wait for payment before sending purchased items. But some individuals or small businesses involved in online sales might be less careful. In these instances, the seller might send the item before receiving payment—and payment never comes.

37

Money Mules

Looking to make some extra money, Karl, a 38-year-old former cabdriver from Grass Valley, California, answered a help wanted ad in April 2005 for a "correspondence manager." The job description said that he would receive packages at home, then reship them overseas. For his efforts, the ad promised to pay him $24 per package shipped. After he applied online, Karl quickly received an e-mail saying he got the job. What he did not know, was that he had just been recruited to be a money mule for an online financial predator.

Money mules help cybercriminals convert stolen personal and financial data into goods and cash. First, the cybercriminals order goods with stolen credit card numbers. Because shipments made within the United States are rarely reviewed once the online transaction has been approved, the criminals recruit unwitting US residents to receive the goods. The money mules then reship the goods to an overseas address where the goods are usually sold on the black market. John Pironti, a security consultant who specializes in bank systems, says cybercriminals are using money mules in an online high-end fencing operation. The mules help them move stolen property overseas where it is difficult to trace.

Many mules, like Karl, do not realize that they are helping cybercriminals. Many times they answer a job listing on a legitimate website such as Monster.com or Jobfinder.com. According to Paul Krenn, a spokesman for the US Postal Inspection Service, cybercriminals find it easy to recruit US citizens because so many are looking to earn extra money.

In 2009 Pennsylvania resident Daniel Moore went online to Craigslist to purchase tickets for the Stanley Cup Finals between the Pittsburgh Penguins and the Detroit Red Wings. He contacted the seller through e-mail and agreed on a price for the hard-to-find hockey tickets. Moore sent a credit card payment to the seller, who promised to leave the tickets at the Detroit arena's ticket office. When Moore arrived, no one at the ticket office had received his tickets or had heard of the seller.

Investment and Charity Scams

Investment and charity scams are other common types of online fraud. Investment scams often lure people with promises of large returns and payouts. In a typical scenario, a financial predator sends an e-mail to potential targets telling them about an investment opportunity. Sometimes, the predator sets up phony websites to convince targets that the business is legitimate. Once recipients send money, the so-called investment opportunity disappears along with the person who sent the pitch.

Online charity scams prey on the generosity of people, especially after a disaster. Financial predators pretend to represent a charity collecting online donations for a worthy cause. Sometimes they use names or URLs that are similar to legitimate nonprofit organizations. Because the urge to help others is powerful, this type of scam often succeeds.

Within hours of Haiti's devastating 2010 earthquake, dozens of legitimate organizations began collecting online donations for the Haitian people. At the same time, online scammers jumped into action to take advantage of the situation and trick unsuspecting donors. Symantec, a security software company, said that spam and phishing e-mails asking for donations usually start within about 24 to 48 hours after a disaster like Haiti's. "We have also seen a few spam campaigns that mention the disaster in Haiti and we expect to see more scams that will use the event to trick people into giving up money,"[45] Joris Evers of McAfee security software said shortly after the quake.

Phishing

Another type of online financial scam, phishing, begins with an e-mail, instant message, or pop-up message. The message instructs the recipient to take immediate action in order to avoid a negative consequence such as a bank account being closed. Often, the message appears to come from a legitimate bank, store, or company. It instructs the victim to log on to a bogus website or call a phone number where the victim will be asked to verify personal information such as Social Security number, credit card numbers, or bank accounts and passwords. Sometimes phishing e-mails contain an attached file that launches malicious software, or malware, when opened. The malware may record keystrokes or data such as e-mail addresses and send the information to the predator. Sometimes malware allows the predator to control the victim's computer remotely for a future attack.

Regardless of how the attack occurs, financial predators gain access to information that allows them to steal money, identity, or both. Investigators report that phishing scams typically yield a positive response rate of 1 to 5 percent. "This statistic is staggering considering a spammer's ability to send out literally hundreds of thousands of e-mails in a matter of minutes,"[46] says Carlson.

> "Identity theft has always been with us—forever. The Internet is making it grow at an exponential level. There are all kinds of scams out there. Now it's just easier."[48]
>
> —Chris E. McGoey, a professional security consultant.

Jeri Smith, a 57-year-old sales consultant from Midland, Michigan, experienced this sort of scam in July 2005. She received an e-mail that told her to click on a link and upgrade her eBay account for security reasons. When she did, the link took her to a site that appeared to be legitimate. There, Smith verified her personal and financial information. Once she had entered the information, Smith realized that she had been scammed. "I could almost kick myself for doing that," she says. "I've been preaching to my mother that she shouldn't answer one of these and then I turn around and give these guys my soul before I think about what I'm doing."[47] Immediately, Smith contacted her bank and changed her PIN number. She also notified her credit card company. The next month, the credit card company called her to report that someone had tried to charge several computers and video games to her account.

Identity Theft

Long before computers, thieves stole bank account numbers from paper statements and credit cards from purses and then went on spending

Dozens of legitimate organizations collected online donations to help the Haitian people after an earthquake destroyed much of the island nation in 2010 (pictured). The disaster also opened the door to online scammers who sought donations under false pretenses.

sprees. Today the Internet has created new avenues for financial predators to steal identities. "Identity theft has always been with us—forever. The Internet is making it grow at an exponential level. There are all kinds of scams out there. Now it's just easier,"[48] says Chris E. McGoey, a professional security consultant based near Los Angeles.

One type of malware, called spyware, tracks every keystroke made on the computer from entry of online passwords, personal information, and account numbers. Usually, the user never knows that keystrokes are being recorded. The spyware then sends this information to the financial predator, who uses it to commit identity theft. The predator can apply for credit cards in the user's name and charge purchases, withdraw money from the user's bank accounts, and take on the user's identity online.

In other cases, financial predators construct phony websites that trick unsuspecting victims into entering personal information. They might sell a small product or service and then steal the user's information. Usually, the user has no way of knowing how or where his or her identity was stolen. Ryan Thomas, an airman in the Air Force Honor Guard, purchased some DVDs on the Internet in 2007 and used his debit card to make the $20 payment. The next day, his $900 bank account was empty. Someone had stolen his account information and used his bank account to buy computer games and other items. "I didn't know better about securing your information on the computer,"[49] Thomas told a *Washington Post* reporter.

Recovering a stolen identity can be difficult for a victim. Dave Crouse suspects that his identity was stolen by keystroke malware that infected his computer. When Crouse, who lives in Bowie, Maryland, noticed suspicious charges on his bank statement in February 2009, he notified his bank and filled out affidavits swearing that he was not responsible for the charges. "At that point I was going to the bank every day and looking at everything,"[50] he told a MarketWatch reporter. Even when he closed the account and opened a new one at a different bank, predators still managed to hit Crouse's account. Unemployed, the financial mess even hurt Crouse's job search. One recruiter told him that they turned him away because his credit reports were so bad and his debt was too high. "It affected me. It affected my livelihood. It affected my whole family,"[51] says Crouse.

Cybercrime Hits Companies

In addition to striking individuals, financial predators also target corporate networks, trying to steal company and customer information. Stolen information of this sort is sometimes sold on the black market to people who hope to use it for their own financial gain, or it might be put to immediate use by the original hacker/thief. To break company network security, hackers have developed a formidable arsenal of computer malware that looks for weaknesses in network defenses.

Malicious attacks on corporate networks are rising in frequency. According to a 2010 data breach report from the Ponemon Institute, 31 percent of data breach cases in 2010 involved a malicious or criminal

Online Car Scams

With a limited budget, Amanda Hanson turned to the Internet to find a car that she could afford. She searched online and discovered a website for America Auto Sales. The site advertised repossessed cars at bargain prices. Although the deals seemed almost too good to be true, the site looked legitimate. It had a link to CarFax, a well-known service that provides used car vehicle history reports. In addition, Hanson researched the company and found that it had an "A" rating from the Better Business Bureau. Satisfied that the company was legitimate, Hanson picked out a car and wired a $2,000 deposit per the site's instructions. What Hanson did not realize was that the website was fraudulent, a cover for financial predators looking to scam car buyers.

After Hanson wired her money, the website quickly disappeared. The thieves had stolen the identity of a real car dealership and set up the website, using its name, address, and information. After the criminals moved on, the real car company was left to deal with more than 1,000 calls from scammed buyers who had lost thousands of dollars. Unfortunately, scams like this are becoming more common. In 2009 the FBI received almost 6,900 consumer complaints about Internet auto fraud.

act, an increase of 7 percent over 2009. In addition, malicious attacks are some of the most expensive to remedy, costing companies an average of $318 per record.

In April 2011 Sony Corporation discovered that a hacker had penetrated its online gaming and entertainment network. The thief stole names, addresses, and possibly credit card data belonging to 77 million user accounts in one of the largest Internet security heists to date. After Sony learned of the break-in, it temporarily shut down its PlayStation network. Even so, the data breach may put millions of Sony customers at risk for identity theft for years.

Although Sony has not disclosed details of the breach, Alan Paller, research director of the SANS Institute, a computer security research and education organization, believes that it probably occurred when the hackers sent an e-mail to a Sony system administrator that contained malicious software. When the employee opened the e-mail, it downloaded the software onto a company computer and allowed the hackers to enter the Sony network and access sensitive information.

Tackling Financial Predators

Several agencies in the United States investigate online financial crimes. The FBI investigates a variety of Internet crimes, including computer hacking, fraud, and identity theft. The FBI also works in partnership with the National White Collar Crime Center at the Internet Crime Complaint Center (IC3). Established in 2000, IC3 is a place for law enforcement agencies at various levels to share information and pursue cases such as phishing or e-mail spam that cross multiple jurisdictions. In 2010 the IC3 received more than 300,000 complaints. IC3 investigated about 170,000 of the complaints and referred those cases to the appropriate local, state, or federal law enforcement agencies to pursue. For the cases not referred, IC3 analyzed them for valuable information to identify emerging fraud trends.

> "Organized, international criminal rings can only be confronted by an organized response by law enforcement across international borders, which we have seen in this case."[53]
>
> — George S. Cardona, acting US attorney.

The United States Secret Service also has an Electronic Crimes Task Force. This group investigates and prosecutes online financial crimes, often in coordination with law enforcement agencies such as local police departments and the FBI. Local and state law enforcement agencies often receive the first reports of online financial crime and open the initial investigations.

Regardless of the agency handling the case, an online financial crime investigation begins with determining where and how the criminal obtained the victim's personal information. Knowing how the crime was committed may help investigators identify suspects and other victims. Investigators also comb through the victim's financial records, statements, and related papers looking for patterns or clues that might lead to the criminal's identity.

A nationwide effort to educate the public about identity theft included this poster, unveiled during a news conference in Maine. Identity theft results when personal information, including bank account and credit card numbers, is stolen and then used for various financial transactions.

Toughening Laws

The increasing complexity of online financial crime has led to the passage of various laws since the 1980s. Although some computer crime fell under existing wire and mail fraud laws, new laws were needed. In response, Congress passed the Comprehensive Crime Control Act of 1984 and the Computer Fraud and Abuse Act of 1986, which include provisions that cover the unauthorized access and use of computers and computer networks. Later amendments to these acts would add provisions to penalize those who used computers to intentionally alter, damage, or destroy data belonging to others or those who trafficked in passwords and other similar personal information.

By the late 1990s the federal government specifically addressed identity theft. The 1998 Identity Theft and Assumption Deterrence Act made identity theft a federal crime and allowed law enforcement to investigate identity theft and its resulting fraud. Those convicted under the act could be imprisoned for up to 15 years and fined a maximum of $250,000.

Ten years later, President George W. Bush signed the Identity Theft Enforcement and Restitution Act of 2008 into law. Previously, prosecutors needed to show that hackers and cybercriminals had caused a minimum of $5,000 in damage before they could prosecute a case. The 2008 act eliminated that requirement, making it easier for identity theft victims to win compensation for their financial loss and time spent fixing their damaged credit and accounts.

> "Cyber crime might not seem real until it hits you. . . . And given the extent of the damage cyber attacks can cause, it is important for all of us to protect ourselves, and each other."[54]
>
> —FBI director Robert Mueller III.

Many states have also enacted laws to protect citizens against online financial predators. For example, restrictions on the use of Social Security numbers as identifiers in public and private documents have been enacted by states. In addition, a majority of states require companies that have been hacked to notify the people whose personal information may have been stolen. "The law applies to businesses and state government agencies that maintain databases when there is a breach involving the acquisition of information such as Social Security numbers, credit card numbers, drivers licenses, and other vulnerable personal information,"[52] says Democratic New York State Assembly member James Brennan.

Using Technology to Catch Online Financial Predators

Some financial institutions have attempted to reduce online financial crime by using more sophisticated technology to trap and thwart would-be predators. Some set up dummy accounts to trap phishers. Others use early detection tools that are designed to spot and shut down fraudulent e-commerce and banking sites before they are finished being constructed.

Internet security companies such as Internet Identity and NexLabs have developed software that analyzes spam for phishing and scans the Internet for fraudulent sites. In addition, many banks and credit card companies now monitor their customers' spending habits. When an unusual charge pops up, they will contact the customer to verify its accuracy.

Operation Phish Phry

In 2009 the FBI announced that nearly 100 people in the United States and Egypt were charged with fraud as a result of Operation Phish Phry, one of the largest cyberfraud phishing cases in history. Egyptian members of the crime ring used e-mails to lure customers of several banks to phony bank websites where they conned the victims into entering their user names and passwords. The criminals then used that information to transfer money from the victims' bank accounts into new accounts that had been set up by their US partners. According to the FBI, the group is suspected of conning several thousand people and illegally transferring more than $1.5 million dollars in a scam that ran from January 2007 through September 2009.

Investigating a large multijurisdictional case like Operation Phish Phry requires the coordination of multiple law enforcement agencies. During the two-year investigation led by the Los Angeles FBI office, the FBI worked closely with the Secret Service Electronic Crimes Task Force in Los Angeles, state and local law enforcement, and Egyptian law enforcement counterparts. "This international phishing ring had a significant impact on two banks and caused huge headaches for hundreds, perhaps thousands, of bank customers. Organized, international criminal rings can only be confronted by an organized response by law enforcement across international borders, which we have seen in this case,"[53] says acting US attorney George S. Cardona.

Despite the operation's success, FBI director Robert Mueller III cautions the public that stopping online cybercrime takes effort from everyone. "Just as the police cannot come by every home or business, every night, to make sure the doors are locked, we must all take ownership of cyber security. Cyber crime might not seem real until it hits you. . . . And given the extent of the damage cyber attacks can cause, it is important for all of us to protect ourselves, and each other."[54]

A Daunting Task

Investigating and prosecuting online financial crime can be challenging for even the most experienced law enforcement officers. There are no witnesses, crime scenes, or fingerprints. Instead, financial predators commit their crimes in obscurity and often thousands of miles away from their victims. As Mueller explains,

> The perpetrators can be anyplace in the world. And so can the victims. And, for that matter, the evidence. At a minimum, piecing together a case requires close collaboration with our counterparts in other countries. But actually prosecuting one requires harmonizing different criminal justice systems, all of which work according to the laws of their own lands. The global scale and scope of such attacks puts law enforcement at a disadvantage.[55]

In addition, identifying victims of online financial crime can be tricky. The first victim is the user whose personal information has been stolen. Banks and credit card companies, however, also become victims when they reimburse customers for fraudulent charges and assume the financial loss. Companies can also be victims of financial fraud if corporate networks are breached to access employee or customer data. Coordinating and gaining the cooperation of all levels of victims can sometimes be difficult for online crime investigators. Some individuals or companies may not want to allow law enforcement access to personal and financial records needed to investigate the crime.

Despite the difficulty in tracking and prosecuting online financial predators, many officials believe that cybersecurity should be one of the nation's top priorities. In a 2009 speech about the importance of cybersecurity, President Barack Obama said,

It's about the privacy and the economic security of American families. We rely on the Internet to pay our bills, to bank, to shop, to file our taxes. But we've had to learn a whole new vocabulary just to stay ahead of the cyber criminals who would do us harm—spyware and malware and spoofing and phishing and botnets. Millions of Americans have been victimized, their privacy violated, their identities stolen, their lives upended, and their wallets emptied.[56]

Chapter Four

Cyberbullies

Sometimes the most vicious online predators are people a user knows. When 15-year-old Phoebe Prince moved from a small Irish village to a Boston suburb, she looked forward to going to an American school. She enrolled at South Hadley High School, where her principal called her smart and charming. Before long, the young girl's Irish accent and wide smile caught the eye of the school's star football player, and the two became romantically involved.

Yet not everyone was happy that Phoebe had come to South Hadley High. A group of girls were upset by the attention the newcomer received. They began to relentlessly torment and bully Phoebe, calling her an "Irish slut" and threatening her. Quickly, the bullying moved online, with taunting text messages and harassing postings on Facebook. "The real problem now is the texting stuff and the cyberbullying. Some kids can be very mean towards one another using that medium. Apparently the young woman had been subjected to taunting from her classmates, mostly through the Facebook and text messages,"[57] says South Hadley school superintendent Gus A. Sayer.

On January 14, 2010, Phoebe hanged herself in an apartment stairwell. Many believe that the relentless cyberbullying was a factor in her decision to take her own life. Even after her death, the cyberbullying did not stop. When some of Phoebe's classmates set up a memorial on an Internet site, the bullies posted insults and slurs. After Phoebe's death, classmate Becky Brouillard said that cyberbullying in the form of texts and online posts was part of teen life at South Hadley High. "A lot of people say stuff anonymously . . . so you don't even know who's saying it. They can talk over a keyboard but they'll never say it to your face,"[58] she said.

Bullies Move Online

Cyberbullying occurs when a bully uses the Internet, cell phones, video game systems, or other digital technologies to threaten or harass another person. Cyberbullying can happen in many forms, from threatening text messages to web pages that make fun of a person. Today's teens go online for schoolwork and to chat with friends, play games, and share pictures or videos. With so many teens online, cyberbullying has become a growing problem. According to the National Crime Prevention Council, approximately 40 percent of teens have experienced some form of cyberbullying.

Because the online world has become a major part of teen life, many are not surprised that some people are using digital technologies to harass others. "Social interactions have increasingly moved from personal contact at school to virtual contact in the chat room. Internet bullying has emerged as a new and growing form of social cruelty,"[59] write Kirk R. Williams and Nancy G. Guerra, researchers at the University of California at Riverside.

The Internet makes bullying devastatingly quick and easy—and anonymous. Hiding behind fake screen names and anonymous e-mail addresses, bullies can mask their true identity from victims. In a 2007

Students hold a candlelight vigil for Phoebe Prince, a Massachusetts high school freshman who killed herself in 2010 after being tormented by her classmates. According to one student, cyberbullying in the form of mean texts and online posts was common at Prince's high school.

Free Speech or Cyberbullying?

When Florida high school senior Katherine Evans became frustrated with her English teacher in 2007, she logged on to her Facebook account and wrote a rant against the teacher. She invited her friends to post comments about their "hatred" of teacher Sarah Phelps. A few days later, Evans took down the post and returned to her graduation preparations. Two months after her Facebook post, Evans's principal called her to the office and told her that she was being suspended for cyberbullying.

The school district believes that Evans's post on Facebook went too far. "You can express an opinion on whether someone is a good teacher," said Pamela Brown, assistant director for the Broward County School District who oversees expulsions. "But when you start inviting people to say that they hate a teacher, that crosses the line."

Others disagree. "Since when did criticism of a teacher morph into assault? If Katie Evans said what she said over burgers with her friends at the mall, there is no question it would be protected by free speech," said Howard Simon, executive director of the American Civil Liberties Union of Florida.

Evans is now suing the principal for suspending her. She is not asking for monetary compensation, only to have the incident removed from her permanent record.

Quoted in Carmen Gentile, "Free Speech or Cyberbullying?," *New York Times*, February 8, 2009. www.nytimes.com.

report by the National Crime Prevention Council, nearly half of teens said that cyberbullying happened because the bully did not think there would be any consequences or felt that he or she would not get caught. The Internet also lowers inhibitions. It is easier to be cruel when a bully does not have to look his or her target in the face. Even worse, cyberbullying can quickly go viral, spreading from phone to phone or computer to computer as people forward or share hurtful messages or join in an attack. Victims feel as if everyone knows or is against them.

"We're always talking about protecting kids on the Internet from adults and bad people. We forget that we sometimes need to protect kids from kids,"[60] says Parry Aftab, executive director of WiredSafety.org.

A Wide Variety of Attacks

The ways a cyberbully can harass a victim are limited only by his or her creativity. Experienced hackers can break into a victim's e-mail or social networking account, hijack it, and send out mean or embarrassing messages while pretending to be the victim. In Ipswich, Massachusetts, an unknown cyberbully hijacked a high school class officer's Facebook page in 2011 and sent out e-mails targeting 22 female students. The e-mails listed the victims' ages, body types, and sexual experience level. Others create entire websites designed to make fun of a classmate or teacher. In Texas, a group of middle school students created a website called deborahisabigfatcow.com. On the now-defunct site, they edited pictures of their victim's face to put it on the body of cows.

> "Social interactions have increasingly moved from personal contact at school to virtual contact in the chat room. Internet bullying has emerged as a new and growing form of social cruelty."[59]
>
> — Kirk R. Williams and Nancy G. Guerra, researchers at the University of California at Riverside.

Cyberbullies harassed 14-year-old Olivia Gardner with an "Olivia Haters" web page that classmates had posted on MySpace. On the page, they called her horrible names and threatened to beat her up. As reported in a 2007 *Washington Post* article about the cyberbullying, one girl posted, "I wish she'd just leave Hill (Middle School) and never come back."[61] Eventually, the cyberbullying became so bad that Olivia transferred schools.

Cyberbullies frequently use e-mail, instant messaging, or text messages to send threatening messages to a victim. Hours after 14-year-old Amanda Marcuson reported that classmates had stolen a pencil case filled with makeup, the harassment began. When she arrived home from school, instant messages popped up calling her a liar and a tattletale. After she tried to defend herself, the messages grew increasingly mean, calling her a "stuck-up bitch" and other names. That night, while at a basketball game with her family, Amanda received 50 nasty messages on her cell phone. "It seems like people can say a lot worse things to someone online than when they're actually talking to them,"[62] Amanda told a *New York Times* reporter.

Cyberbullies sometimes trick victims into sending personal and embarrassing information or pictures, then forward it to other people. Sometimes, even excluding a person from an online group or blocking his or her e-mail can be a form of cruel cyberbullying. Online lists that

Young people who flock to social networking sites to keep up with friends sometimes also use those sites for cyberbullying. Social networking sites offer easy communication but can also be abused.

rate girls as "hot" or "ugly" are another way that cyberbullies harass victims. At Horace Greeley High School in Chappaqua, New York, one list included the names, phone numbers, and details about the sexual encounters of dozens of girls.

Effects of Cyberbullying

Cyberbullying victims may experience many of the same effects as teens who are bullied face-to-face, including loss of self-esteem, low grades, or loss of interest in activities. According to the National Crime Prevention Council, one in eight students felt scared enough from cyberbullying to stay home from school.

Cyberbullying is potentially more harmful than face-to-face bullying. When bullying happens online, teens cannot escape. The harassment follows them home on cell phones and home computers. Online bullying can also spread fast and far. A bully can forward an embarrassing message or picture to hundreds of people within minutes. In addition, psychologists say that the Internet allows users to say things without seeing the effect on others, which can lead to more vicious harassment. When bullies hide behind anonymous posts or e-mail accounts, victims can feel even more insecure. "Individuals can be more isolated when bullying occurs by cell phone or computer. The mechanism for cyber bullying is 'I'm making fun of you; I could have made a photo of you that's not even true and it can go to Facebook.' The audience is much greater. That can be devastating—not knowing how many people have seen that text message or photo,"[63] says Ronald Iannotti, a researcher at the Eunice Kennedy Shriver National Institute of Child and Human Health Department.

> "We're always talking about protecting kids on the Internet from adults and bad people. We forget that we sometimes need to protect kids from kids."[60]
>
> — Parry Aftab, executive director of WiredSafety.org.

A 2010 study by researchers at that institute found that teenage victims of cyberbullying were more likely to suffer from depression than their tormentors. "Notably, cyber victims reported higher depression than cyber bullies or bully-victims, which was not found in any other form of bullying," the study authors wrote in the *Journal of*

the impact of their actions, Hansen says his school was able to reduce its bullying problem.

Drawing a Line on School Responsibility

The majority of state and local cyberbully legislation makes schools responsible for developing and enforcing policies to prevent cyberbullying. Yet many schools find little guidance on how to implement these policies or financial help to pay for new programs and training. School officials say that instructions about what actions they should take in routine cyberbullying cases are often unclear. "I feel significant compassion for, and totally understand, the difficult situation principals are in. The legal standards are unclear, and if [school leaders] don't have a policy that addresses cyberbullying, they end up getting in an argument with parents,"[67] says Willard.

> "The vast majority of cyberbullying incidents can and should be handled informally: with parents, schools, and others working together to address the problem before it rises to the level of a violation of criminal law."[73]
>
> — Justin Patchin, associate professor of criminal justice and and codirector of the Cyberbullying Research Center at the University of Wisconsin–Eau Claire.

When students use off-campus computers to cyberbully, the responsibility issue becomes murky. School officials are unsure whether off-campus cyberbullying falls within the reach of school discipline or if it should be handled by parents or police. The courts have set a prior standard that schools can punish students for off-campus behavior if the behavior includes harassment of students or teachers that threatens their safety or causes a substantial disruption to the school environment. Eric C. Sheninger, principal of a New Jersey high school, says that most school officials believe they should address cyberbullying whether it occurs on or off campus. "We have to act because of the effect it has impacting students' emotional well-being. If students don't feel emotionally safe or comfortable in school, it's going to impact their ability to focus and engage with other students,"[68] he says.

Even in the courts, school responsibility is blurred. Two similar 2010 cyberbullying cases received different court rulings. In both cases students used an off-campus computer to create a fake profile of a school principal on a social networking site. Also in both cases the principals suspended the offending students. In *Layshock v. Hermitage School District*, a three-judge panel sided with the student and upheld an earlier court's ruling that the school district did not demonstrate that the fake profile substantially disrupted the school environment. Yet in *Snyder v. Blue Mountain School District*, a different three-judge panel from the same court ruled that the school district was right to suspend the student because the school had reason to believe that the student's fake profile would substantially disrupt the school. "The real issue here is whether public schools have the legal authority to deal with actions that occur off premises, in off hours, at a non-school-sanctioned event,"[69] says Aftab.

Making Cyberbullying a Criminal Offense

Some people believe that cyberbullying is such a serious offense that simply suspending or expelling students is not tough enough. Instead, they are calling for cyberbullying to be made a criminal offense. Because cyberbullying can have devastating consequences, some believe punishment should be severe. "The law must evolve to address how our society communicates, promoting proper conduct, and deterring future bullying with a legal means to punish those who cause harm,"[70] says Daniel Gelb, a former prosecutor and Boston lawyer.

In 2008 representatives introduced the Megan Meier Act to the US House of Representatives. In 2006, 13-year-old Megan Meier killed herself after receiving mean messages on a social networking website from a classmate's parent who pretended to be another teen. If passed, the act would impose criminal penalties for cyberbullying and would give prosecutors the authority to prosecute users who send online message that are meant "to coerce, intimidate, harass, or cause emotional distress." If convicted, a defendant could face a fine and jail time. "The Megan Meier Act would give prosecutors the tools to protect kids from the most egregious of online predatory attacks,"[71] says one of the bill sponsors, Representative Kenny Hulshof from Missouri.

Critics of the bill question if it violates the Constitution. "I don't even think that's plausibly constitutional. Congress has a completely undistinguished track record of passing impulsively unconstitutional laws when it comes to new technologies,"[72] says Bruce Sanford, a First Amendment lawyer. As an example, Sanford points to federal laws that have attempted to police Internet decency but have been consistently overturned in the courts. Other critics say that a federal law is not needed because state regulations already cover cyberbullying. As of 2011 the bill had expired without being voted on by Congress. It may be reintroduced in a future session of Congress.

Some people do not support a federal law against cyberbullying. "The vast majority of cyberbullying incidents can and should be handled informally: with parents, schools, and others working together to address the problem before it rises to the level of a violation of criminal law,"[73] says Justin Patchin, associate professor of criminal justice and codirector of the Cyberbullying Research Center at the University of Wisconsin–Eau Claire.

> "Bullying has been around forever, but the Internet and social networking sites now give bullies easy access to a worldwide stage to spread rumors and make nasty comments about their targets."[77]
>
> — John Sancin, former president of CyberPatrol.

Sameer Hinduja, codirector of the Cyberbullying Research Center, says that some laws that criminalize cyberbullying may not deter adolescents. "You have to remember that they're students and their development is immature, and they don't consider ramifications. We're villainizing these adolescents for basically screwing up, and we've all screwed up,"[74] he says.

Responsibility Rests at Home

While schools and communities struggle to define their roles in preventing cyberbullying, many people believe that the real responsibility to stop cyberbullying starts with parents educating their children about appropriate online behavior. While some parents support the schools' efforts and disciplinary decisions, others try to pass off student online behavior as a harmless joke. "One of the biggest challenges I face is parents who

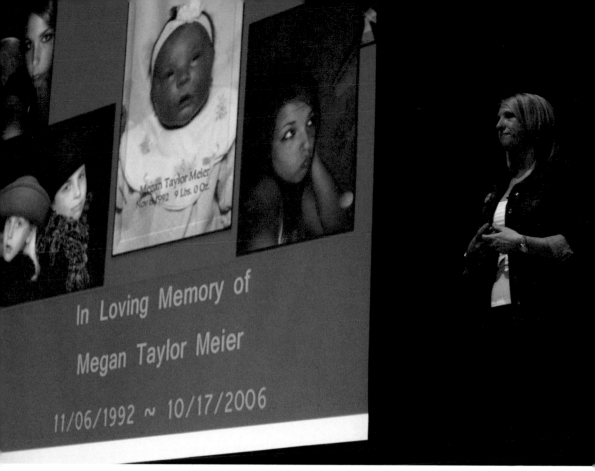

Tina Meier, whose 13-year-old daughter, Megan, hanged herself after being cyberbullied in 2006, speaks to high school students in Pennsylvania about the dangers of cyberbullying. Schools are among the many organizations trying to stamp out such behavior.

try to downplay the bullying as if it's not occurring, and try to talk their way around it,"[75] says Jason C. Briggs, the principal of St. Gregory the Great School in Hamilton Square, New Jersey.

Even parents who want to be involved may feel intimidated by the constantly changing technology that today's teens use to communicate. Although some attempt to keep up with their teens, many do not. "I'm not seeing signs that parents are getting more savvy with technology," says Russell A. Sabella, former president of the American School Counselor Association. "They're not taking the time and effort to educate themselves, and as a result, they've made it another responsibility for schools. But schools didn't give the kids their cell phones."[76]

With teens embracing the digital world for everything from socializing to shopping, it is not surprising that bullies are also using digital technology to attack. Says web-monitoring software developer John Sancin,

Bullying has been around forever, but the Internet and social networking sites now give bullies easy access to a worldwide stage to spread rumors and make nasty comments about their targets. The Internet magnifies this long-time problem. My parents used to tell me that sticks and stones could break my bones, but words could never hurt me. In today's world, I'll take the sticks and stones. An online bully attack is much worse. And the results, as we have seen, can include suicide.[77]

Chapter Five

What Lies Ahead?

Keeping up with online predators is no easy task. The Internet changes constantly as do the ways in which people use it. All of these changes present new and varied opportunities for online predators. "Law enforcement must be aware that technology is continually advancing and that the criminal element will adopt new technology as it comes along. It's not like fingerprints, where you can train someone once and they can lift prints for the next 20 years,"[78] says James Doyle, president of Internet Crimes, a high-technology training company in Madison, Connecticut.

Mobile Devices

Experts predict that online predators will increasingly use mobile devices such as cell phones and smart phones to lure victims. With a smart phone that has Internet access, teens can log in to chat rooms, social networking sites, or send and receive e-mails and text messages at any time or place. For sexual predators and cyberbullies, increased access to victims through mobile technology more easily isolates victims from friends and family, an important step in grooming a victim. Because monitoring a teen's interactions with the Internet community on a smart phone is more difficult, mobile technology leaves teens vulnerable to an online predator's advances anywhere or anytime.

Mobile technology is also an emerging arena for financial predators. As PC makers build better security into computers, predators are turning their attention to newer and less secure mobile devices. According to the *Cisco 2010 Annual Security Report*, online financial predators have begun shifting their focus from Windows-based PCs to smart phones, tablet computers, and mobile platforms in general. "If the bad guys can get a link to arrive on your phone, disguised as if it's coming from Facebook, and get you to click on it, they've got you. It's just as trivial to install a banking Trojan on your smart phone, including iPhones and Droids, as it is on a PC,"[79] says Fred Touchette, a researcher for AppRiver, an Internet security company.

In particular, the mobile apps store is a new way for cybercriminals to reach millions of users quickly. In 2010 millions of users discovered that free wallpaper apps downloaded from the Android market were collecting unnecessary information such as mobile phone numbers and subscriber identification codes. This personal information was then being forwarded to an unknown recipient in China. "Third-party mobile apps are emerging as a serious threat vector. . . . No one is looking at these apps and determining what is a 'good app' or a 'bad app,'"[80] says Horacio Zambrano, product line manager for Cisco.

> "Law enforcement must be aware that technology is continually advancing and that the criminal element will adopt new technology as it comes along."[78]
>
> — James Doyle, president of Internet Crimes, a high-technology training company in Madison, Connecticut.

Social Networks

Almost since their inception, online social networks have been a place where sexual predators groom victims and cyberbullies terrorize targets. These sites have also become a new way for financial predators to scam unsuspecting victims. The size of social networks and the trust a user places in messages from family and friends makes social network an ideal place for financial predators to attack. If users click on tainted Facebook links, they might unknowingly download a program that infects their computers and installs malware.

According to Internet security experts, social network users can expect more threats to spread virally and infect everyone on a user's friend list. These viruses will most likely steal a user's personal information, which can then be used to obtain credit card and banking information. Alternately, stolen personal information could be sold on the black market to

Smart phones and other new mobile devices with quick and continuous Internet access provide additional avenues for online predators of all types. Even mobile apps can turn out to be online scams for unsuspecting consumers.

other financial predators. "Malware and scams that target Facebook users are a very common occurrence in today's threat landscape. With upwards of 500 million users, cybercriminals will continue to target Facebook users and abuse the Facebook brand itself as the social engineering lure in their various criminal schemes,"[81] says Dave Marcus, director of McAfee Labs Security Research Communications.

In 2011 links falsely reporting actor Charlie Sheen's death appeared on Facebook. When users clicked on the link, they were taken to a fake YouTube page, where any click on the page launched the virus on the user's Facebook profile. Some users reported being infected with malware after visiting the fake site. "We have seen an absolute huge rise in malware worldwide over the past 12 months, probably more than the previous five years combined," says David DeWalt, McAfee's chief executive. "We are seeing a lot more malware specifically designed and targeted at large social networking applications. These are just the trends in the industry."[82]

Cybergangs

Because large amounts of money are to be made in online scams, the FBI warns that hackers and other cybercriminals are turning into career online criminals. As they join together, cybergangs are becoming more professional and specialized organizations. Each member focuses on one piece of the gang's operations. Coders or techies maintain the infrastructure such as servers and ISPs, while hackers probe for application and network vulnerabilities to attack. Fraudsters create phishing and spam schemes, and money mules execute wire or bank transfers to move stolen money for the gang. "They make so much money and have so many connections, that they no longer need a legitimate day job. This specialization has been extremely beneficial to cyber criminals,"[83] says deputy assistant FBI director Steven Chabinsky.

To investigate organized cybercrime and infiltrate cybergangs, the FBI uses long-term sting operations and undercover special agents. In one sting operation that ended in 2008, FBI special agent J. Keith Mularski used the screen name "Master Splyntr" and spent two years working with a cybergang known as the Dark Market. Gang members were cautious around the undercover agent at first, but he eventually gained their trust and was admitted into their criminal forum. Mularski says,

> We developed the persona of a spammer/hacker and I assumed that role. Our intention was to try to penetrate the groups and dismantle them like we would with organized crime. In this case we were very successful in getting to the upper echelons of the Dark Market group and we were actually able to run the server and host all the communications that were going on there to make our cases against the criminals.[84]

The undercover agent became so entrenched in the gang that members even ignored a warning that he was a federal agent.

New Safeguards and Defensive Technologies

To protect against more complex and powerful cyberthreats, individuals and organizations are looking to stronger computer and Internet defenses. To slow down cyberrobberies, banks and other online financial institutions use more knowledge-based authentication questions. These questions are an extra layer of security on top of traditional user names and passwords. The authentication questions may ask "What is the name of your first pet?" or "What street did you grow up on?" The questions are designed to be so personal that it would be very difficult for a criminal impersonating a user to answer correctly. "The questions are going to get more difficult over time. The threat is real, and [banks] are providing the tools to help customers protect themselves,"[85] says Doug Johnson, the American Banking Association vice president of risk-management policy.

Some financial institutions are also considering implementing new technologies to make online transactions more secure. Handheld optical readers are one type of new technology that might better protect customers from online predators. The size of a credit card, the optical reader fits into a wallet like a banking card. To use the card, the user presents the card in front of his or her computer screen. Optical sensors capture the card's data to authorize banking transactions. No keypad strokes are needed. Using this type of verification device would help banks and users verify "secure transactions no matter what is on the customer's PC,"[86] says Paul Beverly, executive vice president at Gemalto, a German company that makes optical readers.

Emerging Careers

With rising cybercrime, computer-savvy experts are needed more than ever to investigate computer crime and secure the Internet from online predators. The federal government, education officials, and military contractors are working together to encourage young computer experts to consider careers in cybersecurity and forensics. The FBI has more than 1,000 cybersecurity experts across the United States and in 2010 was looking to boost their ranks. The bureau has also added computer forensics training as a core requirement for all special agents in their Quantico, Virginia, training program.

The emerging field of computer forensics combines elements of law and computer science. A computer forensic investigator recovers, analyzes, and presents data from computers, servers, and laptops that will be used in investigations or as evidence. Computer forensic experts often determine how intrusions into computer systems occurred, recover data from encrypted or deleted files, and recover deleted data. These professionals have detailed knowledge of both computer systems and the legal system. As the number of digital devices increases, computer forensic investigators also search USB flash drives, smart phones, and cell phones.

Vernon D. is a computer forensic detective for a city police department. When working a case, he might obtain a search warrant to seize digital devices such as cell phones, computers, and cameras. Some of his cases include identity theft, financial fraud, and sex crimes against youth. "My favorite part of the job is finding evidence that can confirm or deny that a crime was committed. If it is confirmed, the bad guy goes to jail; if it's denied, an innocent person is cleared,"[87] says Vernon.

The Computer Security Group, based at the University of California at Santa Barbara (UCSB), boasts an assortment of professors, researchers, and students who have teamed up to pursue online criminals. Led by computer science professor Richard Kemmerer, these hacking professionals strive to make research work in the real world. "UCSB is one of the top research centers in the country and world in cybersecurity. Dick Kemmerer and his colleagues have accumulated a large pool of talent that produces very good research results to really important problems. There are only a few schools worldwide with the same level of competence,"[88] says Virgil Gligor, a professor at Carnegie Mellon University in Pittsburgh.

> "We are seeing a lot more malware specifically designed and targeted at large social networking applications. These are just the trends in the industry."[82]
>
> – David DeWalt, McAfee's chief executive.

In 2010 the Computer Security Group succeeded in taking over a botnet named Torpig. A botnet is a network of hijacked home computers, sometimes called zombies, that criminals hide behind and use to send spam, infect other computers, or commit crimes. The team watched the botnet's operations for 10 days. During that time, the botnet accumulated 60 gigabytes of personal data, including 900 credit card numbers and more than 400 bank accounts. The team turned over the information to the FBI.

Kemmerer notes that law enforcement agencies, particularly the FBI, the Department of Homeland Security, and NASA's Computer Crimes Division have welcomed working with his group. "They need all the help they can get," he explains. "These guys are trying to prosecute people, and for that, they need the evidence. People like us can collect the evidence for them—even better if we can analyze and come up with insights they didn't get. It's a freebie for them. I think they're overwhelmed. There is so much cyber crime out there."[89]

Cooperation Across Borders

The Internet has broken down borders around the world, allowing people from different states and countries to interact, do business, and communicate more easily than ever. At the same time, online predators can strike from anywhere, anytime. Cybergangs do not need to be physically located together; instead, they can operate from countries around the world. Law enforcement experts say that the key to fighting cybercrime is international cooperation.

In Operation Trident Breach, which began in May 2009, FBI and law enforcement agents from several countries worked together to disrupt an international cybercrime operation. The criminals infected computers of businesses, municipalities, and individuals with malware that captured passwords, account numbers, and other data used for online banking. With the stolen information, they attempted to steal $220 million. To stop the cybercrooks, the FBI worked closely with international agencies to identify and arrest suspects involved in the operation. Assistant Director Gordon M. Snow of the FBI's Cyber Division credited the cooperation among the different agencies and countries with being critical to the investigation's success.

> **"The bottom line is to make sure there are consequences for criminal cyber actions and similar consequences everywhere. The bad guys need to know there is no free ride."[90]**
>
> — Christopher Painter, deputy assistant director of the FBI's Cyber Division.

While timely cooperation is important, Christopher Painter, deputy assistant director of the FBI's Cyber Division, says that laws against cybercrimes need to be consistent from state to state and country to country. If not, criminals will simply learn to base their operations in jurisdictions where penalties are the least severe. "The bottom line is to make sure there are consequences for criminal cyber actions and similar consequences everywhere. The bad guys need to know there is no free ride,"[90] says Painter.

International Treaty

In a step toward international cooperation, the Council of Europe introduced a treaty called the European Convention on Cybercrime in 2001. The treaty establishes guidelines for sharing data between governments in cases of bank fraud, identity theft, child porn, phishing, and other kinds of online organized crime. Forty-six countries, including the United States, have signed the treaty. Some US conservatives worry, however,

As part of Operation Trident Breach, an international effort to stop cybercrime, the FBI released a poster showing cybercriminals from Eastern Europe who are wanted on a variety of federal charges stemming from money laundering, bank fraud, passport fraud, and identify theft in New York. The key to stopping cybercrime, experts agree, is international cooperation.

that the treaty is a step toward world government, blurring the lines of national sovereignty. They point out that it would commit the FBI and US law enforcement to track down evidence of international crimes that are not US crimes. Supporters of the treaty argue that it has provisions that let member countries reject information requests. For example, the FBI would be able to turn down an information request from China about dissident bloggers in America.

Some countries, such as Russia, are reluctant to sign the international treaty. Russia, considered to be a major source of cybercrime, says it does not want to give foreign law enforcement agents unlimited access to its web data, which the treaty requires. Alternatively, Russia has proposed an arms-control treaty in which all nations would agree

Wi-Fi Investigator

In cybercrime investigations, attempts to trace a hacker's digital footprint back to a wireless network often lead to a dead end. To operate, many times cybercriminals will log on to the poorly protected wireless networks of neighbors or businesses. Investigators can trace their cyberattacks back to the point of origin, the wireless network, but not to the specific mobile device connected to that network. Without the ability to locate the device connected to the wireless network, investigations may stall.

A new tool from cybersecurity company Digital Certainty might help solve this problem. Wi-Fi Investigator is a wireless device locator that allows police to physically locate active wireless devices. When a cybercrook logs on to a wireless network, Wi-Fi Investigator can conduct surveillance on the activity. It can also calculate GPS coordinates of the device's location, leading police right to the crook.

not to use cyberweapons. "There are a lot of controversial issues that need to be resolved before we can sign that convention," says Vladislav Sherstuyuk, who leads the Institute of Information Security Issues at Moscow State University. Russia wants to "preserve state sovereignty and monopoly on the conduct of investigative activities based on existing domestic laws and procedures,"[91] he says. Critics point out that it would be nearly impossible to define cyberweapons and determine whether a government or an individual hacker was responsible for a cyberattack.

To ensure that all countries are taking cybercrime seriously, US lawmakers introduced the International Cybercrime Reporting and Cooperation Act in 2010. If passed, the act would require the president to report annually to Congress on cybercrime emanating from each country and the effectiveness of that country's legal and law enforcement systems. It would also identify countries of cyberconcern, where significant, credible evidence that a pattern of cybercrime against the

United States exists. If those countries did not actively address their cybercrimes, the United States could impose a variety of economic sanctions. Says Senator Orrin Hatch of Utah, one of the bill's cosponsors:

> Cybercrime is a serious threat to the security of the global economy, which is why we need to coordinate our fight worldwide. Until countries begin to take the necessary steps to fight criminals within their borders, cybercrime havens will continue to flourish. We don't have the luxury to sit back and do nothing. I believe the International Cybercrime Reporting and Cooperation Act will not only function as a deterrent of cybercrime, but will prove to be an essential tool necessary to keep the Internet open for business."[92]

A Complex Age

All over the world, people are logging on to computers and the Internet. In many ways, digital technology has improved daily life and work. Access to information and communication with a variety of people is easier than ever. Surfing the Internet on laptops, computers, and mobile devices, people can read the latest news and research almost any topic in minutes. With e-mail, instant messaging, and social networking, people thousands of miles apart can communicate, share ideas, and learn about different cultures.

At the same time, the Internet and the digital age have opened the door to new vulnerabilities and problems. In this evolving and complex world, online predators have found new ways to find victims and commit crimes. Sexual predators lure teens in chat rooms and use webcams to reach into a victim's bedroom. Financial predators have learned to steal banking account information and passwords with a few keyboard clicks. And cyberbullies are using digital technology to harass their victims more viciously than ever.

> "Cybercrime is a serious threat to the security of the global economy, which is why we need to coordinate our fight worldwide."[92]
>
> — US senator Orrin Hatch of Utah.

To minimize these risks, governments, law enforcement agencies, and communities around the world are working to educate and design new procedures and technologies that better protect against online predators. With all of these ongoing efforts, Kemmerer remains optimistic about the future: "It's not going to be totally secure, but there are enough of us good guys that I'm sure the bad guys aren't going to win. But the bad guys are always going to be there."[93]

Introduction: Dangers Online

1. Quoted in Joe B. Crowe, "Facebook Case Helps Fight Cybercrime," *Birmingham News*, April 19, 2009. http://blog.al.com.
2. Quoted in Crowe, "Facebook Case Helps Fight Cybercrime."
3. Quoted in Jacque Kochak, "New Face of Internet Stalking Is Local," *Auburn Villager*, April 24, 2009. www.auburnvillager.com.
4. Quoted in Kristen DiPaolo, "Internet Predators," Connect with Kids, March 15, 2006. www.connectwithkids.com.

Chapter One: A Real Problem

5. Quoted in Carolyn Salazar, "How Dangerous Is Online Banking?" *MSN Money*, January 28, 2009. http://articles.moneycentral.msn.com.
6. Quoted in CyberPatrol, "Proliferation of Cyber Bullying and Cyber Predators Prompts Need for Better Online Protection for Kids," press release, March 9, 2010. www.cyberpatrol.com.
7. Janis Wolak, David Finkelhor, and Kimberly Mitchell, "Trends in Arrests of Online Predators," Crimes Against Children Research Center, 2009.
8. Quoted in David Muir, "All Children Vulnerable to Online Predators," ABC News.com, April 6, 2006. http://abcnews.go.com.
9. Quoted in *Consumer Reports Magazine*, "When Sharing Goes Too Far," June 2010. www.consumerreports.org.
10. Linda Criddle, *Look Both Ways: Help Protect Your Family on the Internet*. Redmond, WA: Microsoft Press, 2006, p. 6.
11. Criddle, *Look Both Ways*, p. 9.
12. Quoted in *Clarksville Online*, "Teens Still Share Alarming Amounts of Personal Information Online," June 24, 2010. www.clarksvilleonline.com.
13. Quoted in Carrie-Ann Skinner, "Majority of Web Users Share Personal Data Online," *Computerworld*, August 12, 2008. www.computerworld.com.
14. Quoted in Bill Brubaker, "Online Records May Aid ID Theft," *Washington Post*, January 2, 2008. www.washingtonpost.com.

15. Quoted in Brubaker, "Online Records May Aid ID Theft."
16. Living and Learning with New Media: Summary of Findings from the Digital Youth Project, "Digital Youth Project," November 2008. http://digitalyouth.ischool.berkeley.edu.
17. Quoted in CyberPatrol, "Newly Formed CyberPatrol to Help Families Protect Themselves from Online Threats," press release, April 2, 2008. www.cyberpatrol.com.

Chapter Two: Sexual Predators

18. Katie Canton, "Katie's Story," *Human Sexuality Newsletter*, vol. 36, no. 4, December 2009.
19. Canton,"Katie's Story."
20. Euripol, "More than 200 Children Identified and Rescued in Worldwide Police Operation," March 16, 2011. www.europol.europa.eu.
21. Quoted in David Singleton, "Darkness on the Web: Tracking Online Predators," *Times Tribune* (Scranton, PA), September 26, 2010. http://thetimes-tribune.com.
22. Quoted in Susanna Schrobsdorff, "Predator's Playground," *Newsweek*, January 27, 2006. www.newsweek.com.
23. Quoted in L. Alvin Malesky Jr.,"Predatory Online Behavior: Modus Operandi of Convicted Sex Offenders in Identifying Potential Victims and Contacting Minors over the Internet," *Journal of Child Sexual Abuse*, vol. 16, no. 2, 2007, pp. 23–32.
24. Quoted in Schrobsdorff, "Predator's Playground."
25. Quoted in Edmund H. Mahony, "Camp Counselor Pleads Guilty in Child 'Sextortion' Case," *Hartford Courant*, January 26, 2011. http://articles.courant.com.
26. Quoted in Gwen Florio, "Missoula's Internet Task Force Fights Crimes Against Children," *Missoulian*, November 21, 2010. http://missoulian.com.
27. Quoted in LiveFiveNews, "AG's Internet Predator Task Force Marks 200th Arrest," November 19, 2010. www.live5news.com.
28. Quoted in *Vanity Fair*, "A Crime of Shadows," no. 592, December 2009, p. 244.
29. Quoted in Laurence Hammack and Lindsey Nair, "Epidemic or Easy Target?," *Roanoke Times*, November 19, 2006. www.roanoke.com.
30. Quoted in Businesswire.com, "MySpace Uses Sentinel SAFE to Provide All 50 States Valuable Intelligence on Registered Sex Offenders," May 21, 2007. www.businesswire.com.

31. Quoted in CNN.com, "MySpace Kicks out 90,000 Sex Offenders," February 3, 2009. http://articles.cnn.com.

32. Quoted in Marlon Walker, "Facebook Gives Sex Offenders the Boot," MSNBC.com, February 19, 2009. www.msnbc.msn.com.

33. Quoted in Walker, "Facebook Gives Sex Offenders the Boot."

34. Quoted in Stephanie Reitz, "Facebook, States Set Predator Safeguards," MSNBC.com, May 8, 2008. www.msnbc.msn.com.

35. Quoted in *Curriculum Review*, "Initiative Geared Toward Stopping Internet Predators," vol. 48, no. 1, September 2008.

36. Quoted in Holden Frith, "Facebook: Parents Are Responsible for Child Safety Too," *Times*, April 4, 2008. http://technology.timesonline.co.uk.

37. Quoted in Tanya Roscorla, "Social Media Sparks School Policy Debate," *Ecology of Education*, July 22, 2009. http://ecologyofeducation.net.

38. Quoted in Roscorla, "Social Media Sparks School Policy Debate."

39. Quoted in Mike Musgrove, "Challenging Assumptions About Online Predators," *Washington Post*, January 25, 2009. www.washingtonpost.com.

40. Quoted in Musgrove, "Challenging Assumptions About Online Predators."

41. New York State Senate, "Senator Joe Robach and Attorney General Cuomo Announce 'e-stop' Legislation," March 26, 2009. http://www.nysenate.gov.

Chapter Three: Financial Predators

42. Quoted in Byron Acohido, "Banks Seek Customers' Help to Stop Online Thieves," *USA Today*, July 30, 2010. www.usatoday.com.

43. Quoted in Acohido, "Banks Seek Customers' Help to Stop Online Thieves."

44. Quoted in Mark Reutter, "Internet Opens New Avenues for Con Artists Seeking to Bilk the Elderly," University of Illinois at Urbana–Champlain, March 23, 2007. http://news.illinois.edu.

45. Quoted in Suzanne Choney, "Beware of Bogus Online 'Help' for Haiti," MSNBC.com, January 13, 2010. www.msnbc.msn.com.

46. Quoted in Reutter, "Internet Opens New Avenues for Con Artists."

47. Quoted in Brian Krebs, "It's 10 PM. Do You Know Where Your Identity Is?," *Popular Mechanics*, Feburary 2006.

48. Quoted in Andrea Neal, "Guarding Against Identity Theft," *Saturday Evening Post*, vol. 279, no. 3, May 2007, p. 48.

49. Quoted in Allison Klein, "18- to 24-Year-Olds Most at Risk for ID Theft, Survey Finds," *Washington Post*, March 17, 2010. www.washingtonpost.com.

50. Quoted in Jennifer Waters, "Identity Fraud Nightmare: One Man's Story," MarketWatch.com, February 10, 2010. www.marketwatch.com.

51. Quoted in Waters, "Identity Fraud Nightmare."

52. Quoted in Rene Millman, "New York Enacts Data Break Law," *SC Magazine*, August 15, 2005. www.scmagazineus.com.

53. Quoted in FBI Los Angeles, "One Hundred Linked to International Computer Hacking Ring Charged by United States and Egypt in Operation Phish Phry," press release, October 7, 2009. http://losangeles.fbi.gov.

54. Robert Mueller III, "Cloak and Dagger in the Virtual World," speech, Commonwealth Club of California, San Francisco, CA, October 7, 2009. www.fbi.gov.

55. Mueller, "Cloak and Dagger in the Virtual World."

56. Barack Obama, "Remarks by the President on Securing Our Nation's Cyber Infrastructure," May 29, 2009. www.whitehouse.gov.

Chapter Four: Cyberbullies

57. Quoted in Kathy McCabe, "Teen's Suicide Prompts a Look at Bullying," *Boston Globe*, January 24, 2010. www.boston.com.

58. Quoted in Alyssa Giacobbe, "Who Failed Phoebe Prince?" *Boston Magazine*, May 23, 2010. www.bostonmagazine.com.

59. Quoted in Tara Parker Rope, "More Teens Victimized by Cyber Bullies," *New York Times*, November 27, 2007. http://well.blogs.nytimes.com.

60. Quoted in Amy Harmon, "Internet Gives Teenage Bullies Weapons to Wound from Afar," *New York Times*, August 26, 2004. www.nytimes.com.

61. Quoted in Ilene Lelchuck, "School Bullies' New Turf: Internet," *Chronicle*, March 17, 2007. www.sfgate.com.

62. Quoted in Harmon, "Internet Gives Teenage Bullies Weapons to Wound from Afar."

63. Quoted in *Science Daily*, "In Cyber Bullying, Depression Hits Victims Hardest," September 26, 2010. www.sciencedaily.com.

64. Quoted in Traci Pedersen, "Depression High in Cyber Bully Victims," PsychCentral.com, September 22, 2010. http://psychcentral.com.

65. Quoted in Ashley Surdin, "In Several States, a Push to Stem Cyber-Bullying," *Washington Post*, January 1, 2009. www.washingtonpost.com.

66. Quoted in Michelle R. Davis, "State Cyberbullying Laws Range from Guidance to Mandate," *Education Week*, February 4, 2011. www.edweek.org.

67. Quoted in Michelle R. Davis, "Schools Tackle Legal Twists and Turns of Cyberbullying," *Education Week*, February 9, 2011. www.edweek.org.

68. Quoted in Davis, "Schools Tackle Legal Twists and Turns of Cyberbullying."

69. Quoted in Davis, "Schools Tackle Legal Twists and Turns of Cyberbullying."

70. Daniel Gelb, "Privacy Invasions Last Forever," *New York Times*, September 30, 2010. www.nytimes.com.

71. Quoted in eSchool News, "Federal Lawmaker Targets Cyber Bullying," May 27, 2008. www.eschoolnews.com.

72. Quoted in eSchool News, "Federal Lawmaker Targets Cyber Bullying."

73. Justin Patchin, "Most Cases Aren't Criminal," *New York Times*, September 20, 2010. www.nytimes.com.

74. Quoted in Davis, "State Cyberbullying Laws Range from Guidance to Mandate."

75. Quoted in Davis, "Schools Tackle Legal Twists and Turns of Cyberbullying."

76. Quoted in Jan Hoffman, "As Bullies Go Digital, Parents Play Catch-Up," *New York Times*, December 4, 2010. www.nytimes.com.

77. Quoted in CyberPatrol, "CyberPatrol Empowers Parents with Free Online Tools to Combat Cyber-Bullying," press release, April 6, 2010. www.cyberpatrol.com.

Chapter Five: What Lies Ahead?

78. Quoted in Paul Roberts, "Experts Search for Ways to Fight Cyber-crime," *PC World*, February 12, 2003. www.pcworld.com.

79. Quoted in Byron Acohido, "Zeus Banking Trojan Attacks Spread to Social Networks, Smartphones," *USA Today*, October 8, 2010. http://content.usatoday.com.

80. Quoted in CISCO, *Cisco 2010 Annual Security Report*, p. 34. www.cisco.com.

81. Quoted in Tony Bradley, "Protect Your Network from Facebook Malware," *PC World*, August 20, 2010. www.pcworld.com.

82. Quoted in Judi Hassan, "Facebook Gets Serious About Malware," Fierce CIO.com, January 13, 2010. www.fiercecio.com.

83. Quoted in Kenneth Corbin, "FBI Underboss Says Cyber Criminals the New Mafia," eSecurity Planet, March 23, 2010. http://www.esecurityplanet.com.

84. Quoted in Elinor Mills, "Q&A: FBI Agent Looks Back on Time Posing as a Cybercriminal," CNET News, May 7, 2009. http://news.cnet.com.

85. Quoted in Alejandro Gonzalez, "Banks Seek Customers' Help to Stop Online Thieves," *USA Today*, July 30, 2010. www.usatoday.com.

86. Quoted in Gonzalez, "Banks Seek Customers' Help to Stop Online Thieves."

87. Vernon D., "Computer Forensic Analyst Interview," All Criminal Justice Schools. www.allcriminaljusticeschools.com.

88. Quoted in Matt Kettmann, "Just the Hackers You Need," *Santa Barbara Independent*, December 16, 2010. www.independent.com.

89. Quoted in Kettmann, "Just the Hackers You Need."

90. Quoted in *North Country Gazette*, "International Cooperation Needed to Fight Cyber Crime," January 14, 2009. www.northcountrygazette.org.

91. Quoted in Homeland Security Newswire, "To Avoid Cyberwar and Protect Infrastructure—Fight Cybercrime First," April 14, 2010. http://homelandsecuritynewswire.com.

92. Quoted in "Cybercrime Costs NY Businesses Approximately $4.6 Billion Each Year—Gillibrand, Hatch Introduce First of Its Kind Measure to Bolster Cybersecurity in America," press release, Senator Kirsten Gillibrand, March 23, 2010. http://gillibrand.senate.gov.

93. Quoted in Kettmann, "Just the Hackers You Need."

Facts About Online Predators

- In 2010 identity theft was the top consumer complaint received by the Federal Trade Commission.

- According to Javelin Strategy & Research's 2011 Indentity Fraud Survey Report, 8.1 million adults in the United States were identity fraud victims in 2010.

- The *New York Times* reported that the average consumer out-of-pocket cost due to identity fraud increased to $631 per incident in 2010.

- The Anti Phishing Working Group says that more than 53 percent of desktop computers are infected with some type of malware.

- According to a recent Gallup poll, in 2010, 11 percent of Americans said they or someone in their household had been the victim of a computer or Internet-based crime.

- According to a 2009 Gallup crime survey, identity theft is American's top crime worry, with 66 percent of adults reporting that they worry frequently or occasionally about being a victim of identity theft.

- According to a Gallup poll, 48 percent of Americans report using the Internet more than one hour per day.

- A Zogby International poll found that 44 percent of teens believe the information they put online is secure, but 79 percent say their friends share too much information online.

- According to the *2010 Symantec Internet Security Threat Report*, the average daily volume of web-based attacks observed in 2010 was 93 percent higher than in 2009.

- According to research by the Pew Internet & American Life Project, 15 percent of teens report having private material such as e-mails, texts, or instant messages forwarded without permission.

- Girls report more online harassment than boys do. Thirty-eight percent of girls report some form of online harassment, says the Pew Internet & American Life Project.

- According to the US Department of Justice, Internet Crimes Against Children task force investigations led to more than 3,100 arrests of online sexual predators in 2008.

- According to the University of New Hampshire's Crimes Against Children Research Center, 4 percent of youth online are asked within a year to transmit a sexual picture of themselves.

- According to the Crimes Against Children Research Center, violence occurs in only 5 percent of cases involving online sexual predators. In most encounters, victims meet offenders voluntarily.

- According to the Crimes Against Children Research Center, most Internet sex crimes involve youth ages 13 to 15.

- The Crimes Against Children Research Center reports that 1 in 25 youth (4 percent) received aggressive online sexual solicitations that included attempts to meet offline.

Center for Safe and Responsible Internet Use (CSRIU)

474 W. 29th Ave.
Eugene, OR 97405
phone: (541) 556-1145
e-mail: contact@csriu.org
website: www.cyberbully.org

The CSRIU provides consulting services to school districts, administrators, and school attorneys related to Internet use, cyberbullying, and sexting. Its website provides information and resources for students, parents, and educators.

Federal Bureau of Investigation (FBI) Cyber Crime Division

935 Pennsylvania Ave. NW
Washington, DC 20535-0001
phone: (202) 324-3000
website: www.fbi.gov

The FBI's Cyber Crime Division investigates high-tech crimes, including cyber-based terrorism, computer intrusions, online sexual exploitation, and major cyber frauds. Agents gather and share information and intelligence with public- and private-sector partners worldwide.

Federal Bureau of Investigation (FBI) Innocent Images National Initiative (IINI)

935 Pennsylvania Ave. NW
Washington, DC 20535-0001
phone: (202) 324-3000
website: www.fbi.gov

The FBI's Innocent Images National Initiative teams FBI agents with local police around the country in proactive task forces that work online undercover to stop online predators.

International Centre for Missing & Exploited Children (ICMEC)

1700 Diagonal Rd., Suite 625
Alexandria, VA 22314
phone: (703) 837-6313
fax: (703) 549-4504
e-mail: information@icmec.org
website: www.icmec.org

ICMEC is leading a global movement to protect children from sexual exploitation and abduction. ICMEC provides training for law enforcement, prosecutors, and other professionals around the world on how to investigate Internet-related child exploitation cases. ICMEC has also launched a global Internet safety campaign.

Internet Crime Complaint Center (IC3)

website: www.ic3.org

IC3 is a partnership between the FBI, the National White Collar Crime Center, and the Bureau of Justice Assistance. IC3 receives complaints regarding cybercrime and coordinates efforts between law enforcement and regulatory agencies at the federal, state, local, and international level.

Make a Difference for Kids

e-mail: mark@makeadifferenceforkids.org
website: www.makeadifferenceforkids.org

Make a Difference for Kids, Inc., is a nonprofit organization promoting awareness and prevention of cyberbullying and suicide.

National Center for Missing & Exploited Children (NCMEC)

Charles B. Wang International Children's Building
699 Prince St.
Alexandria, VA 22314-3175
phone: (703) 224-2150
fax: (703) 224-2122
CyberTipline: (800) 843-5678

NCMEC offers a CyberTipline for reporting possible illegal Internet activity related to child pornography, online predators, or other types of child sexual exploitation.

National Cyber-Forensics & Training Alliance (NCFTA)
2000 Technology Dr., Suite 450
Pittsburgh, PA 15219
phone: (412) 802-8000
fax: (412) 802-8510
e-mail: info@ncfta.net
website: www.ncfta.net

The NCFTA functions as a conduit between private industry and law enforcement to identify, mitigate, and neutralize cybercrime. NCFTA currently has formal partnership agreements with more than 40 US private-sector organizations and more than 15 US and international law enforcement or regulatory agencies.

Pew Internet & American Life Project
1615 L St. NW, Suite 700
Washington, DC 20036
phone: (202) 419-4500
fax: (202) 419-4505
website: www.pewinternet.org

The Pew Internet & American Life Project is one of seven projects that make up the Pew Research Center, a nonpartisan, nonprofit "fact tank" that provides information on the issues, attitudes, and trends shaping America and the world. The project studies the Internet and digital technologies shaping the world today.

United States Postal Inspection Service (USPIS)
Criminal Investigations Service Center
Attn: Mail Fraud
222 S. Riverside Plaza, Suite 1250
Chicago, IL 60606-6100
phone: (877) 876-2455
website: https://postalinspectors.uspis.gov

The USPIS is the law enforcement arm of the US Postal Service. Many fraud schemes that originate over the Internet, such as auction fraud, involve payment or delivery via the US Mail and are under the jurisdiction of the USPIS.

Web Wise Kids

PO Box 27203
Santa Ana, CA 92799
phone: (866) 932-9473
fax: (714) 435-0523
e-mail: info@webwisekids.org
website: www.webwisekids.org

Web Wise Kids is a national nonprofit organization that empowers today's youth to make wise choices online. The organization supplies Internet safety tips and games to help youth learn Internet safety skills.

Wired Safety

phone: 201-463-8663
e-mail: parry@aftab.com
Web site: www.wiredsafety.org

A nonprofit organization that is one of the largest online safety, education, and help groups worldwide, Wired Safety operates through more than 9,000 volunteers who patrol the Internet looking for child pornography, child molesters, and cyber stalkers. The group also offers educational programs and services for communities.

For Further Research

Books

Martin T. Biegelman, *Identity Theft Handbook: Detection, Prevention, and Security*. Hoboken, NJ: Wiley, 2009.

Thomas A. Jacobs, *Teen Cyberbullying Investigated: Where Do Your Rights End and Consequences Begin?* Minneapolis, MN: Free Spirit, 2010.

Samuel McQuade III, James P. Colt, and Nancy Meyer, *Cyber Bullying: Protecting Kids and Adults from Online Bullies*. Santa Barbara, CA: Praeger, 2009.

Corey Sandler, *Living with the Internet and Online Dangers*. New York: Checkmark, 2010.

Alexis Singer, *Alexis: My True Story of Being Seduced by an Online Predator (Louder than Words)*. Deerfield Beach, FL: HCI Teens, 2010.

Internet Sources

Internet Crime Complaint Center, "2010 Internet Crime Report," 2011. www.ic3.gov/media/annualreport/2010_IC3Report.pdf.

KidsHealth.org, "Safe Surfing Tips for Teens." http://kidshealth.org/teen/safety/safebasics/internet_safety.html.

Amanda Lenhart, "Cyberbullying 2010: What the Research Tells Us," Pew Internet & American Life Project, May 6, 2010. www.pewinternet.org/Presentations/2010/May/Cyberbullying-2010.aspx.

Kathryn Zickuhr, "Generations and Their Gadgets," Pew Internet & American Life Project, February 3, 2011. www.pewinternet.org/Reports/2011/Generations-and-gadgets.aspx.

Websites

Cyberbullying Research Center (www.cyberbullying.us). The site provides fact sheets, publications, and other research about cyberbullying.

Fighting Back Against Identity Theft (www.consumer.gov/idtheft). This Federal Trade Commission site gives steps to take if you are a victim of identity theft.

Microsoft Safety & Security Center (www.microsoft.com/security/default.aspx). This Microsoft site offers information and tools to help consumers manage a variety of safety and security issues that exist online.

NetSmartz Workshop (www.netsmartz.org). Interactive, educational safety resource from the National Center for Missing & Exploited Children.

SafeTeens.com (www.safeteens.com). This site offers advice to teens and parents about Internet safety.

StaySafeOnline.org (www.staysafeonline.org). From the National Cyber Security Alliance, this site offers information and tools to help people use the Internet safely and securely at home, work, and school.

Index

Picture Credits

About the Author

Carla Mooney is the author of many books for young adults and children. She lives in Pittsburgh, Pennsylvania, with her husband and three children.